Home Is Where the Books Are

Creating Literate Spaces, Choosing Books, & Why It Matters

CHOICE LITERACY
PRODUCTIONS, IN

Meghan Rose & Ruth Shagoury

Choice Literacy, P.O. Box 790, Holden, Maine 04429
www.choiceliteracy.com

Copyright © 2013 by Meghan Rose and Ruth Shagoury

All rights reserved. No part of this publication may be reproduced or transmitted in any form or by any means, electronic or mechanical, including photocopy, or any information and retrieval system, without permission from the publisher.

Every effort has been made to contact copyright holders for permission to reproduce borrowed material. We regret any oversights that may have occurred and will be pleased to rectify them in subsequent reprints of the work.

Library of Congress Cataloging in Publication Data Pending

ISBN 978-1-60155-044-6

Cover and interior design by Martha Drury
Photography by James Whitney
Manufactured in the United States of America

17 16 15 14 13   10 9 8 7 6 5 4 3 2 1

To Molly and Jacob

Contents

Introduction 1

Part I: Setting the Stage 7
Chapter 1: Physical Environment 9
Chapter 2: Growing Up in a World of Reading—and Readers 21
Chapter 3: Media Matters 35

Part II: What to Read 47
Chapter 4: ABCs 49
Chapter 5: 123s 61
Chapter 6: Relate It to ME! 73
Chapter 7: Have Some Fun 87
Chapter 8: Let's Get (Meta)Physical (Books About Books) 95

Part III: Traditions, Rituals, and Celebrations 103
Chapter 9: Family Traditions: The Call of Books 105
Chapter 10: Celebrate Special Days, with Books in Hand 121
Chapter 11: Holidays and Books Go Hand in Hand 147

And the Beat Goes On 167
References *169*
Children's Books *173*

Introduction

Do I Have to Get a Black-and-White Mobile?
Meghan Rose

It began with a simple question. I was seven months pregnant with twins and had been working 15 hours a day when the Internet company I was working for went under. It was kind of a blessing in disguise, as a week later, my doctor put me on strict bed rest. I did what any overeducated, type-A-personality, previously-too-busy-to-do-any-planning-for-the-babies mother-to-be would do. I sat in bed, laptop propped on pillows next to me, researching (and then buying) online everything my children would need until they were two.

Interspersed with acquisitions, I researched parenting philosophies and baby development. Having decided on some of the big things (crib, changing table, bouncy seats, car seats, and so on), I had moved on to minutiae. Like a mobile: Cute little animals? Lights? Sounds? Color? We had been given one by friends who said their baby LOVED this model and would stare at it, burbling happily (and quietly) for hours. Free and road tested? Seemed like we were all set. But it was in bright colors. I kept reading in baby magazines and in toy advertisements that experts said that babies' toys should be in black and white for maximum brain stimulation, since babies can see only black and white. Was the best thing for them really the black-and-white-checkered mobile? I didn't even like that one. It looked stupid, with the grinning floating baby head on one side. One hormone-induced crying fit later I was on the phone with my mother, who is (luckily for me) a researcher, teacher, and writer who specializes in language acquisition. "Mommy," I sobbed, "do I have to get a black-and-white mobile?"

The simple answer was no. Okay, with a teacher for a mom, it's not a quick or simple answer, and we spent a long time talking about why the answer is no, why people think the answer is yes, and how many toy companies have made gobs of money off the commonly held but inaccurate belief. Too often, we've been led to believe that there is a quick solution to everything—available to be purchased online or elsewhere.

Time and time again I would call my mom and ask her if some "universal truth" about language acquisition and brain development was in fact true. Time and time again I would call her to vent frustrations and insecurities I developed after hearing from experts about the right things to do for kids, or even from other parents. And what I learned is this: my instincts are pretty darn good. And that's true of all of us. I mean, that's biology, right? We instinctively know the right things to do for our kids. If books are important to you (and if you're reading this, they are), then you probably have some spot-on instincts about how to raise kids who will be great readers, lifelong readers, absorbed and fascinated readers (not to mention writers). And as a completely awesome side benefit, that love of learning and reading will in fact result in high grades and test scores. (Not something that I personally place importance in, but since I have two kids who will hit college at the exact same time, right about the year 2020, when college will probably cost approximately half a million dollars for each child, I'm willing to be quite grateful if something they love anyway, like reading, makes them good scholarship material.)

I have found myself sharing the information and answers I have gotten from my mom with girlfriends, casual park acquaintances, and now like-minded parents at my kids' school. I feel like I have gained the confidence to trust in my own instincts, and that, in turn, has given me the freedom to play and explore the world of books and literacy with my children. Molly and Jacob are six as we finish writing this book, and already I delight in seeing how much letters, words, books, writing, creating, and art are part of their lives. I'm not an expert, but I'd love to share with you some of the questions I've had, the answers I've discovered, and the games and tips my kids, my mom, and I have come up with in the last few years.

And to back me up with some of the research and science, here's the real expert, my own mum:

Heartbeats
Ruth Shagoury

I remember so well the phone call with the exciting news:

"Mom. [Pause.] I'm pregnant! We heard the baby's heartbeat!"

Then Chuck's voice chimed in on the other line, "And then we heard the other baby's heartbeat."

My baby was having babies? Excitement gave way to images in my head: me in a rocking chair with two babies—and a book. Reading bedtime stories, writing together, perusing library shelves, making our own little books, and . . . Are you noticing a pattern here?

For me—and for Meghan—childhood memories conjure up lots of images of sharing stories—through talk and listening, through reading and writing, and through stacks and stacks of books read, discussed, and recommended. I knew from the start—from that first exciting phone announcement that changed all our lives—that the little twins would be passionate readers. Not because it's "in their genes," but because we would share what it means to be real readers. We wouldn't be able to help ourselves, and growing up in this literate, book-filled environment would feel as natural to Molly and Jacob as it is essential to us.

Because I've spent my adult life researching, teaching, and loving children's literature and the wonders of children's language and exploring ways to connect reading, writing, and talk, it was natural for Meghan and me to extend our talk of all things baby (then toddler, then young child) to a range of issues and contemporary trends in young children's language and literacy development. We shared stories and asked questions, becoming even more fascinated with this miracle of child development.

As a researcher, I've always learned best from case studies—extended, in-depth collections of observations, stories, examples, ongoing questions, and mental meanderings about the learning of one unique person or classroom. Our shared investigations within our family became a kind of case study of raising literate kids in the 21st century. The questions we've had have led us to turn inward, thinking about what has worked for us as people who love to read and write—and they've led us to other experts in the field to check out some of the new learnings—and new myths—that make their way into our daily experiences.

We hope our stories will ring true for you—and that you'll trust your instincts and discoveries as we share what we've been noticing, learning, and having fun sharing. Our "case study" examples of the twins, Molly and Jacob, will, we hope, give you a chance to draw parallels to your own experiences, and to find some practical book suggestions, tips, and a little research to back it all up.

After this introduction, you'll notice the book is written in first-person singular—*I*—from Meghan's perspective. Although we both wrote it, we decided this would make the book more readable and we'd be able to avoid the awkwardness and confusion of two voices in a coauthored text.

Our format for the book is to share stories and tips, and then follow it up with why this matters, including brief descriptions of what current research says, and what to look for in your own kids.

Oh, and by the way . . . here's more about why Meghan didn't need to get a black-and-white mobile for the babies' nursery.

> Babies see color right from the beginning. When you are creating a stimulating environment for your children, feel free to delight in the excitement of color and don't feel restricted to someone's idea of what all babies prefer.

That's not just our opinion, but the pediatric establishment's, too. "Babies see color from the time they are newborns. There have been a lot of studies using color and watching babies' eyes track it," says John Dorsey, MD (2011).

Dr. Jill Sutton (2008), an infant brain development specialist, stresses that infants in particular love colorful, high-contrast images—not just black and white, but vibrant reds and yellows, too. She recommends filling your baby's world with a range of colors. By four to six months, a baby can see a full spectrum of colors, including even subtle pastels.

Growing research confirms that babies as young as four months show a preference for certain colors. "Some babies in particular show a striking preference for just one color," says Surrey Baby Lab researcher Dr. Anna Franklin (May 2005, reported on the BBC News). Across cultures, babies showed similar likes in that they preferred highly saturated, richer colors over de-saturated colors. Brown and gray in particular were considered the least attractive.

This research is also helpful to keep in the back of your mind as yet more support for how incredible babies are and how often they are underestimated. You'll enjoy watching your baby—or babies—as they show their own particular color preferences early on, and you can build on their own special favorites. Are there great books to explore the literary world of color? You bet! We'll be sharing those suggestions—and more—throughout this book.

PART ONE

Setting the Stage

Home is where it all starts. My own childhood homes ranged from the tiny guest apartment where I was born to a rambling (and ramshackle) Victorian house in a shoe factory town, all in various places in rural New England. The one thing they all had in common: books were everywhere. The first thing my parents would do when we moved to a new home was construct floor-to-ceiling bookshelves in most of the rooms in the house (there were even bookshelves in the bathroom!) and unpack the books. My most vivid memories are of being read to by someone who loved me: Gram (my great-grandmother) reading to me when I was three and had pneumonia; Grandpa letting me pick out books to borrow from his library; my dad reading to me from *Little House in the Big Woods* (Wilder 1932); my mom reading *The Tale of Two Bad Mice* (Potter 1904) to me when I could barely walk. We didn't always have a lot of money, but we always had a lot of books.

My favorite place to be was "the big red chair." I learned to read in that reading chair (see Photo 1-1). I read to my cousins and little brother in that chair. That chair is where my brother and I sat at the very edge of the cushions, leaning forward so we

8   Home Is Where the Books Are

Photo 1-1: Meghan learns to read in "the big red chair."

wouldn't miss a word of my parents reading aloud each night from *The Lion, the Witch and the Wardrobe* (Lewis 1950). That's the book that inspired me to take my brother out one day on an adventure and leave behind a note for our parents, which read (in crayon and invented spelling), "Gone to Narnia. Be back same time we left."

That feeling—the books, the chair, the reading, the emotional touch of books being absorbed into your skin and becoming a very part of you—is exactly what I wanted to create (re-create?) for my own kids. So I began at home . . .

CHAPTER 1

Physical Environment

If you want to create a literate kid, you have to start where the baby starts out—your home. Setting the stage and creating a home where literacy thrives is something you can do even before your baby comes into the world. That sounds pretty daunting, and more than a little pretentious. But actually, it just means thinking about the nursery you're setting up, the early toys and books you're filling the house with, and the first interactions and games you can play with your child at home. I thought a good starting place would be to talk about how I set up our home (after placing the brightly colored mobile I wanted over the crib!) to make sure it was a place filled with books and words and letters, share some of the early games we played, and the things I learned along the way, both from my expert mother and soon afterward from my young children.

The environment is more than bookshelves and rocking chairs. It's the toys you have, the games you play, the behavior you model, and even the kinds of literacy you encourage: books, songs, computers, paper and pens, phones, laptops, iPads, e-readers, televisions, and more are all valid forms of literacy and things to consider when raising kids.

As a voracious reader and compulsive writer, it is very important to me to instill in my kids a love of reading, writing, books, and words. I want a home where it feels natural to curl up with a book, write your own story, or even get lost in your own make-believe world. Before the twins were born, I had lots of ideas about what I wanted to do and the way I would do it. After having them, they taught me where I was right, where I was wrong, and how very much I have to learn.

I started with the premise that a good reading environment is one where books and words and letters are found in every room in the house, sprinkled among other toys, and where they can be incorporated into fun and ordinary activities every day. And where everything from the furniture to the lighting to the environment supports literacy activities and explorations. (See Photo 1-2.)

The stories that follow will give you a glimpse of what it's like, at least in our family's environment, when kids and parents are surrounded by books and print and letters and symbols in their everyday activities.

Photo 1-2: Molly and Jacob look at board books in front of their bookshelves.

Chapter 1 **11**

A Special Reading Place

Coming from a family of readers, I can certainly vouch for the fact that anyplace can be a reading place. As a kid, I read in the car, under the covers, and in the bathroom. I fought with my brother over the cereal box at breakfast (just to have something to read at a time and place where books weren't really allowed). Today I'm trying to create that same environment.

But as fun as it is to read anywhere, I've learned that, for young children at least, it's really wonderful to have a special reading place. We have the rocking chair.

When the kids were first born, it was the place for nursing, cuddling, soothing, and, from day one, reading. Until they went to school, we began each day in the rocking chair for stories before breakfast. If a guest in our home (like Grandpa—see Photo 1-3) made the mistake of starting to read to the kids on the floor or the couch, they would shake their heads, take the book away, and lead the errant adult to the rocking chair. Barely able to walk, they already knew it was the place for reading (see Photo 1-4).

Alone, together, or with anyone else, the rocking chair is still their special reading chair. Probably because we all read so much,

Photo 1-3: Grandpa Jim reads to Molly and Jacob.

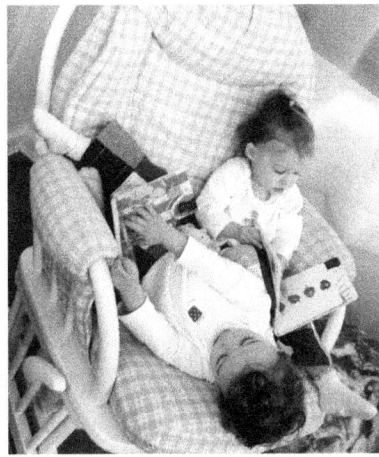

Photo 1-4: Molly and Jacob read in their special rocking chair.

Photo 1-5: This little one is happy on the floor, surrounded by books.

and because it was their first place for food and comfort, it has become a great resource for us when the kids are tired or sick or just overwhelmed. Nothing turns around a cranky day faster than the promise of "any book you want, in the rocking chair."

If you don't have a rocking chair, try picking another special place in your house. If there isn't a convenient chair or couch for reading, it can be a reading blanket that you sit on or curl up under, or some other special thing that signifies to your child that at that time, nothing will come between you and them and a good book. (See Photos 1-5 and 1-6.)

Wet Letters

"Oh, I have so many alphabets in my tub!" two-and-a-half–year-old Jacob said one day in the bath. I pointed to two groups of letters I had arranged.

"Do you know what those are?" I asked, thinking that perhaps I had been doing too much playing with the foam letters,

Photo 1-6: Anyplace can be a fine place to read!

and not enough explaining and talking about individual letters if he was calling them all "alphabets." But he easily identified them. "The letters on top say Molly, and the down low letters say Jacob," he explained, pointing at the names *Molly* and *Jacob* I'd spelled out. He then dumped a pail of water on Molly's head.

I knew it was easy to be playful with the letters of the alphabet. Magnet letters for refrigerators have been a staple "toy" for generations, and I remember playing with them as a child both at home and at my grandparents' houses. At our house we have letters on the fridge, wooden letter puzzles, and nice, fat foam letters that stick to the walls of the tub or shower when they're wet. But after hearing the twins refer to them interchangeably as letters, toys, and alphabets and use them as hats, pretend food, and pretty designs, I worried. Was I doing enough? Was this right? Would they arrive at preschool behind other kids who clearly knew what letters were and how they formed words?

And as always, when I worried, I turned to my mom, who did what moms do best—reassured me. It turns out that even before children know that these brightly colored movable objects are called "letters," they can delight in moving them around, chewing on them, and simply accepting them as part of their environment. Then as they grow, they start to have special attachments to the letters they see more often, like those that start their own names, or *M* for *Mom*. They can learn playfully by simply arranging letters in patterns and enjoying their varying shapes and colors.

Being playful with letters does not hinder their understanding of the alphabet or how to use letters. In fact, it encourages it. It makes letters something that aren't just for grown-ups, but something that even toddlers can work with and manipulate. As I saw with Jacob in the tub, he could understand that letters made words, and could recognize some words that he saw repeatedly. He and Molly also often used fridge magnets and blocks and tub letters to spell out simple words long before they had the fine-motor skills to write them.

Try taking a tour of your own house. Look in each room for something with letters on it. If you can't find something, make it a game to think of what you could place there. Can you leave a set of foam letters in the tub? Nothing in the living room: how about moving the alphabet blocks in there? The dining room is a great place to keep placemats with letters on them, or to remind you to buy some plates or cups with the alphabet or your child's name on them. Alphabet cookie cutters can stay in the kitchen along with the magnets for the fridge. An alphabet puzzle could be in your bedroom, for when they play in there as you put away laundry or bounce on the bed. There's something to tuck away in every room in the house.

I Spy . . . Literacy (A New Game)

About six months after Jacob told me about all the "alphabets" in his tub, I was in the kitchen making dinner. The kids were enjoying their usual raucous play, and since it didn't involve either me or banging on the pots I was trying to cook with, I mostly tuned it out. But when I could finally leave dinner to cook and turned to them, I saw that they had taken all their letter magnets off the fridge and put them all over the kitchen floor behind me. About to bellow at them to "pick this all up before someone slips and gets hurt," I paused, listened, and took a closer look. They weren't making a mess. They were playing a game. "I spy with my little eye . . . a *D*," Jacob yelled.

"Now jump on it," Molly told him. He jumped on the letter and clapped for himself.

"My turn," Mol crowed. "I spy . . ." They played happily, yelling, finding letters and jumping until dinner was ready.

By having letters everywhere in our house, the kids see letters, words, and literacy as something we use as frequently and enjoyably as we do forks, spoons, and knives. They get the subtle message that we really don't have to be limited in the ways in which we use letters. Just as a letter in the tub may make a great hat, the letters on the fridge (or floor) can be turned into a wonderful game. The game could have been played just as easily with colors or objects, but since the letters are present in every room, they picked those out, and ended up playing an educational game that can grow in sophistication as the children do.

Sleeping with Letters

One recurrent theme of motherhood has been sitting back and being surprised at just how much my kids teach me, if I'll let them. As someone who likes to have all the answers, I have found this to be a bit of an adjustment, but a wonderful one.

We moved the twins up to big-kid beds from their toddler beds when they turned five. (I know, on the late side, but they had super-cool toddler beds they were loath to give up!) Their big birthday present from Grandma and Grandpa was picking out new sheets and bedding, and it was on a trip to Pottery Barn Kids that Jacob managed to delight and surprise me again. We steered him away from *Star Wars* (he doesn't know who or what it is, but recognizes the characters from T-shirts) since I thought he'd tire of it quickly, and his eyes lighted up as he saw Dr. Seuss sheets with the alphabet on them.

"Mommy, I can sleep with the letters," he shouted. "Does this have all twenty-six?"

"I'm pretty sure it does, honey, but we can count them when we get home."

And we did. The first week he slept on his sheets, he put himself to bed by inventing different word games every night. One night he'd try to find all the letters in his name. The next night he'd count the letters. The next night he'd say the letter and what it was for (they had illustrations), then move on to all the other words he could think of that began with that letter. And more than one morning he woke up telling me, "Mommy, I slept with my letters and they gave me happy alphabet dreams!"

Now when people tell me that they are thinking of getting flashcards to work with their kids on letters to get them ready for kindergarten, I no longer launch into one of my off-putting rants on how dreadful flashcards are. Instead, I smile and tell them our family secret is pillowcases, not flashcards.

Once you start looking, you'll be amazed at the letters all around us, ready for opportunities to explore and play. Making breakfast? How about pancakes in the shapes of the letters in your kids' names? At the park? There's a world of letters on signs and postings—and another world of letters to see in nature: *Y*s in the tree branches, fluffy *O*s in the clouds, and shapes you can create with long blades of grass, sticks, or lines of stones. Stuck in traffic? It's a great time to look for letters on the sides of trucks, buses, or vans—and to go on treasure hunts for the letters that start the names of family members on the traffic signs and directions along the way.

It's really just a matter of taking stock in your everyday activities and interests and being a bit more intentional in letter explorations. Believe it or not, even a pretty spontaneous and fun game like I Spy is strongly recommended by neurologists (Christian, Morrison, and Bryant 1998). Matching activities like this help kids learn how to discriminate, categorize, and describe objects' characteristics. They also help develop concepts such as same, different, shape, size, and color. The visual discrimination that is encouraged by "searching for a match" of a characteristic is actually a foundational cognitive skill. All that from pillowcases and pancakes.

World of Alphabet Blocks

Molly and Jacob were very into play with letters in the form of magnets and tubby toys, but that childhood staple, the alphabet block, wasn't very popular at our house. That was odd, since they are big builders and love making crazy castles and roads and stacking blocks. Most children enjoy stacking and building wooden cubes well before they notice letters and sounds in the print around them. What finally caught their interest were the sets of beautiful blocks at Grandma's house that were in Spanish and Arabic (as well as the traditional English ones). Mom (Ruth) discovered them when she volunteered at Head Start and met children speaking a dozen different languages learning literacy in a single classroom. (See Photo 1-7.)

Molly and Jacob really loved these blocks. They mixed all the sets together, creating a melting pot of letters and languages, signs and symbols. At first, they didn't realize that many of the blocks had letters on them, but then we talked about the different kinds of letters and languages, and even a little about family heritage. We talked about how their great-grandpa grew up reading and writing in Arabic, which looked nothing like the alphabet to them. We extended the family discussion to talking about another family language that had become part of a family tradition—our Hebrew good-nights. We tuck the kids in three times at night, and after getting bored with saying "One-two-three" I did it in

Photo 1-7: Molly and Jacob play with Arabic alphabet blocks.

French, Spanish, Italian, and pig Latin. That was all I could think of off the top of my head. One night when the kids were about three, Chuck (my husband) said, "Alef, beth, gimel."

"What's that, Daddy?" the kids asked.

"Well, it's Hebrew," he replied. "But I can't remember one-two-three in Hebrew, so that's A-B-C." We talked about different letters in different languages, and who in our family speaks them and why. Since alphabets provide a way of writing language so that oral traditions and histories aren't lost, it's wonderful to use various versions as a starting place to pass on our own family histories to our kids.

Why This Matters …

Creating a literate environment at home sets the stage and expectation for reading as an important part of regular family life.

Although most of the research on instructional environments focuses on *classrooms*, fascinating research demonstrates that the same effects may be found in supportive *home* environments. Having a literate home environment makes books, writing, and literacy in general feel natural to children. Literacy researchers Timothy Rasinski and Anthony Fredericks found that having a literate home develops a love for reading and writing in young children: "A literate home environment doesn't teach children how to read; rather, it provides children with opportunities to enjoy reading and discover the many ways it can be used to enrich the experiences in their lives" (Rasinski and Fredericks 1991, 439).

Dr. Jill Stamm, a researcher in infant and toddler brain development, recommends having special reading places. She stresses that special nooks, chairs, and "reading nests" help create in young children's developing brains a connection between reading and security, enjoyment and literate experiences. She even recommends, if possible, making a special reading place near or in a child's play area, with letters and books a part of that total environment. (See Photo 1-8.)

Dr. Laura Colker, in her suggestions for an ideal literate home environment, has this advice for parents about alphabet letters: "It's important that parents have different types of letters that children can move around, such as magnetic letters for the refrigerator and foam letters for the bathtub. It's also good to have alphabet blocks and puzzles, letter-shaped cookie cutters, letter stamps and stickers. Children love writing their name; these materials give them the opportunity to do so over and over again" (2009).

Photo 1-8: Jacob enjoys a picture book.

It's common sense that alphabet letters support children's literacy. But rather than "teach" the alphabet, literacy specialists recommend that parents and teachers provide many opportunities for kids to playfully and naturally *encounter* the letters, their names, and their sounds.

CHAPTER 2

Growing Up in a World of Reading —and Readers

One of the first things you realize when you become a parent is that you are your child's whole world. It's exhilarating and terrifying. *I am completely responsible for everything this child eats, hears, experiences, and learns for quite a while,* a new mother (or father) thinks, and promptly feels overwhelmed. But here's the easy part: some of what they learn, they'll learn just from watching you. And some of what you want to teach them and instill in them are things you probably already do, or will do naturally as a parent. Read to yourself? You probably love to. (Come on—even if you don't think of yourself as a reader, there's something you love to read, even if it's a magazine, cookbook, or instruction manual!) Read to your child? That's the most natural thing in the world. Listening to your child and showing them your willingness to learn from them and respond to their needs—we do that every day in ways we don't even realize. (I sometimes respond so much on autopilot that I can't remember what I've said, but the kids repeat it to me, and I find that I've said some decent things throughout the day!) By simply reading, listening, and learning, you are taking the first behavioral steps toward raising a reader.

Model Behavior

I'm a reading addict. I love to read. I read constantly. I think about books and what will happen in the one I happen to be in the middle of reading when I should be doing other things (important things, like playing with and listening to my children, driving, working . . .). I stay up late at night to finish a book when I should be getting some much-needed sleep, which leaves me cranky and irritable in the morning. I make my husband crazy by reading surreptitiously in horrible lighting when we're supposed to be watching a movie together. Sometimes I even tell my kids to go away and play because Mommy is really busy—reading the new *Food and Wine* magazine or Rick Riordan book. I don't watch TV to unwind. I'm too busy and exhausted to spend time on the phone catching up with friends as a means of decompressing. My way of relaxing is some me-time with a book.

I used to feel really guilty about this. I even tried to ignore my book cravings, but it only made them worse. I have come to terms with and even embrace my addiction. It was my daughter who made me come to this new way of thinking.

Once when Grandma and Grandpa were in town, we were driving somewhere in the car. We were kind of squished in, and I was invading Molly's personal space more than she liked. She told her grandma that I was in her way, and then in typical Molly fashion, she expounded on that. "Grandma, sometimes I need some alone time, and I have to tell Mommy to go away."

True, very true. But then, in typical Grandma fashion, my mom donned her researcher cap and asked probing follow-up questions. "What do you need alone time for?"

"Well, I have to read books or play or think up stories by myself."

"Do you think Mommy ever needs alone time too?" (Thank you, Mom!)

My little girl didn't hesitate. With the certainty of a four-year-old, who knows that her parents exist only in relation to her, she immediately shook her head. "No. Mommy always needs her little girl."

Seeing me take this time for myself is one of the ways Molly learned that people (in her mind, it's just her, but when she's a little older, she'll learn to extrapolate from herself to the world at large) need alone time, and that reading can give you that mental break. Just as kids need to be read to in order to learn fundamental *physical* book basics (book handling, holding it right side up, that in Western society we track left to right and turn pages the same way) and storytelling basics (Once upon a time . . . They lived happily ever after . . . The end), they need to see *psychological* book basics demonstrated for them as well. I think it's great for them to see that parents are people, that we need breaks, get tired, and have emotions. And sometimes, what we really, really, really want to do is curl up with a great book. A book-reading break for me, especially in the middle of the day, is a treat on par with a gourmet chocolate truffle. My kids have seen that illustrated for them, and though I don't think they'd go so far as to pick a book over chocolate any time soon, they do see books as escapes, refuges, and necessities.

What to Read to a Newborn?

Recently, a friend and I were talking about what books to give a mutual friend (and a big book lover) who is expecting her first baby. We started reminiscing about what we had each read to our own kids when they were newborns. (See Photos 2-1 and 2-2.) "I read *Goodnight Moon* [Brown 1947] of course," my friend said, and then in a confessional tone added, "But I think I read aloud

Photo 2-1: Meghan reads to newborn Molly.

more back issues of *The New Yorker* than anything else. It was the only way I could catch up on them. Isn't that terrible?" Well, no. Far from finding it terrible, I think it's great.

I was reading a book the other day that began, "Literacy begins at birth." I nodded to myself and mentally bookmarked that thought. There is no such thing as reading to a baby too early or too often. We all believe that, right? That's not in question. But how many new parents want to bash their heads into a wall after the 500th reading of *Goodnight Moon*? Is that really all we can read to our newborns? I don't think so.

Photo 2-2: Ruth reads to the twins.

Part of the value of reading aloud comes from the simplest things. From the moment they are born (and even earlier), our children learn to recognize our voices, our language (and pick up on the differences in languages being spoken to them), and even specific words. This isn't something they can learn only from reading aloud the baby classics; this can be learned from *anything* you read aloud.

What you should read is this: anything you like. Be it cookbooks, *The New Yorker*, heck, *People* magazine, or your own favorite book. Between nursing and rocking our twins to sleep in their first year of life, I leaned on the arm of our couch so often, I wore through the fabric on the arm. I tired of the kids' books pretty quickly, so I turned to *A Midsummer Night's Dream* (Shakespeare 2004). I think I read it straight through to the kids five times in a row. It was fun for me, it gave me some beautiful language to concentrate on, and it bizarrely made me feel like I was giving them an early appreciation of Shakespeare.

I ended up buying a mix of books for my expectant friend. I got her *Pat the Bunny* (Kunhardt 2001) (Molly's favorite at an early age), *A Midsummer Night's Dream*, the latest *Entertainment Weekly*, and a personal board book favorite, *Baby, Mix Me a Drink* (Brown 2005). I hope she reads them all to her new little one, and I hope she treasures every one of those reading moments now, before that baby can demand the latest Max and Ruby book for the 93rd time in a row.

Teaching Mommy to Read

Perhaps the only thing more delightful for a reader than doing some reading of your own is watching your children learn to read. One of the most fascinating things about watching Molly and Jacob learn to read is how much it has expanded my definition and understanding of what reading really is.

Molly and Jacob began "reading" books a few months before they turned two. The reason I put *reading* in quotes is merely to clarify what I mean by reading. It consists of taking the books we read hundreds of times a week and reading back to me what they've memorized for each page. At first I thought of this as mere memorizing, but I came to consider it actual reading, and here's why: This isn't pure regurgitation. It includes the shortening or editorializing they've heard from their parents. I was amazed by this (especially the first time Jacob shook his finger at David in *No, David!* [Shannon 1998] and said, "That's it, mister, you stay after school!") and thought it was the way they'd "read" until they actually learned to read. But once I really started paying attention, I realized that putting *reading* in quotes, which I was doing mentally, was wrong. They were really reading.

Memorization is a form of reading—one of the first forms I noticed with the kids. It was also reading when Molly went through a whole book and only told us the background color of each page. She was getting meaning and enjoyment from the book, probably more than when I skim. When Jacob read *The*

Little Fire Engine (Lenski 2000) backward, he wasn't looking for the narrative I would look for, but for how the fire engine works—and he wanted to start with the fire. Makes perfect sense.

The next step seemed to be adding their own storytelling into the mix. For example, when Jacob read *Trucks, Trucks, Trucks* (Sis 2000), he would insert his own experiences into the last page. Matt and his mother go out in the real world to see real trucks, and Jacob would say, "Mommy shower, and then go out." I think he'd heard a few too many times at our house, "First Mommy has to shower and then we can do X."

Molly read *The Three Bears* (Galdone 2011) to me, which starts, "Once upon a time, [there were] three bears." Then she read *The Tale of Peter Rabbit* (Potter 1902), beginning, "Once upon time, three little bunnies." At first, I tried gently correcting her by saying things like, "Yes, there were three good little bunnies and Peter. There were four little bunnies." She kept repeating, "Once upon time, three little bunnies." Then I got it. I heard her reading *Spicy Hot Colors* (Shahan 2007) by saying, "Once upon time, three colors." She read every book with what she considered a proper beginning ("Once upon a time, there were three . . .") and ending ("The end"). The most jaw-dropping moment was when she picked up the book I was currently reading, a paperback mystery novel with small print, and began reading, "Once upon time, three words . . ." (See Photo 2-3.)

I thought I'd be teaching my kids to read. Then I learned that if I paid attention, they were the ones teaching me all about reading.

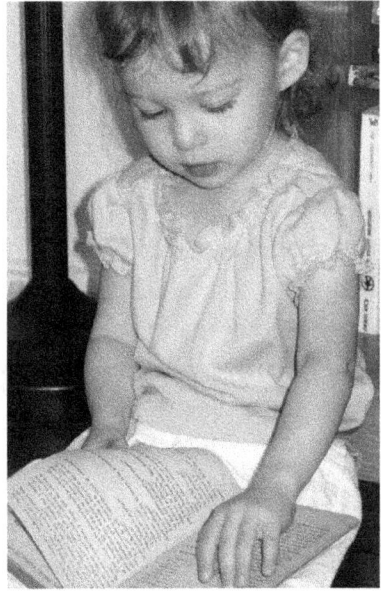

Photo 2-3: Molly "reads" a mystery novel.

Wonderful First Books

You've already got *Pat the Bunny* (Kunhardt 1940) and *Goodnight Moon* (Brown 1947), right? Those *are* wonderful to read aloud. But there are some other books that aren't as well known that really resonated with my own kids as first "read to myself" books. I've given and tested them with friends and asked teachers I know, and these books seem to have universal appeal for the very youngest readers.

First the Egg by Laura Vaccaro Seeger

I had never heard of it, but Mom recommended it as a book the kids in a local Head Start class adore. So we got it out of the library. It's a brightly colored picture book with a few simple words on each page that is predictable and compelling. "First the egg . . . then the chicken," it begins. The development of life is shown from tadpole to frog, caterpillar to butterfly. But we don't stay with nature—we turn to literacy and art with "First the word, then the story . . . ; first the paint, then the picture . . ." We read it to Molly once, and she became *the* expert on this book in our family. After hearing it the one time, she went off in a corner and quietly read the book for ages, then began reading it aloud to us. I know that most of her ability to do that came from the beautiful simplicity of the words and that repetition of the story made it easy for her to memorize. But another part of it was that the pictures also tell the story, so although she remembered the gist, she was actually able to read the book to us by using a combination of memory and the pictures.

The pride you see in your child's face when they read you a book they haven't heard a thousand times definitely made me want to give this book special recognition. If you have prereaders in your house, look for this book and see what they think.

Wave by Suzy Lee

This wordless picture book is a treat, as the simple and beautiful illustrations capture the excitement and awe of a little girl's interaction with the ocean's waves at the beach. From her wonder at the wave, to the playful taunting of the ocean, to the drenching crash, to the discovery of the shells left behind, and finally to the gentle "wave" goodbye, every reader in the family will remember their own favorite times at the beach. The book appeals to a wide audience and is a great book to own, as it also grows with kids. They start by appreciating that they can read the whole book by themselves, then graduate to still enjoying the pictures and soft humor. Even adults will find themselves wishing for framed copies of the illustrations to hang on the walls. It's also a fun "bring-along book." I love having a stockpile of books about things we often do, and find that tucking one into my bag that mirrors our activities and pulling it out for a little snuggle and downtime while we read it helps break up a long day. This book is frequently tucked into our bag as we head to the beach. We also have books that go to the zoo, out for dim sum (or for other types of food . . . each had its own book), to the park, and even on walks around the neighborhood to look at construction sites.

Tip Tip Dig Dig by Emma Garcia

This is a wonderful book about trucks that belongs on every truck lover's shelf. The pictures are bright and bold, the words are repetitive, and the message is positive: when all the trucks work together, they can recycle everything from a dump and turn it into an adventure playground. What I love about this book is that in its simplicity, there is actually a lot to talk about as your truck lover grows. We started out chanting the words ("With the Roller, we can Roll Roll Roll . . .") when we first read the book (when the twins were around 18 months old). Then both kids memorized the book and would read it to me. Next we talked about the different color of each truck, and what each truck does, and how the pieces of trash were recycled. There is a great follow-up book, too, called *Toot Toot Beep Beep*. As I mentioned before, Jacob is a big truck guy, so this one was really more for him. I included it on this list because I know lots of little boys love trucks, but also to illustrate how valuable it is to find a book like this with few words and wonderful illustrations that are about a subject your child adores. I hate that I just wrote that sentence, saying that *boys* like trucks. I don't wish to perpetuate sexist suppositions and stereotypes. But I really have noticed among all the kids we know that in general, the boys love trucks much more than the girls do. Jacob is a far more tender parent to baby dolls than his sister, and Molly and her friends all adore dinosaurs, but trucks seem to be in the boys' domain.

Hello Hello by Dan Zanes, illustrated by Donald Saaf

This book is an illustrated song by kids' musician Dan Zanes (formerly of the Del Fuegos). Our whole family fell in love first with the beautiful, imaginative illustrations, then the music, and finally the lyrics. The kids continue to delight in the pictures and finding new things, but it's the words that stay with me (and that I think will resonate more and more with them), especially the last page, which has "Hello" in several different languages. Nothing makes you smile quite as hard as your toddler cheerily yelling, *"Ni Hao!"* to you in the morning. An extra bonus is the four additional songs on the CD, which will provide you with some parent-friendly kid music. (Have you noticed how much music promises to be just that, but is really the same old annoying kids' music, marketed as "parent-friendly"? But this is truly listenable music!)

It's fascinating as a mom to have the luxury of enough time to pay attention to the different ways the kids read. It helps me understand their process, find books that will appeal to them, and, I hope, understand them better and be a better mother to them. But Molly and Jacob also taught me something that has purely and selfishly benefited me as a reader. I am reminded to read more slowly and find the narrative that speaks to me at that moment in time—in their books, in my books, and in life in general.

The next time you read a story to your child, let him or her lead the way. It's second nature to us to teach, to correct our children, and to show them the "right" way to do things, whether it's reading books from left to right, wanting to read straight through without going backward, not wanting to skip pages, or not turning a page before we're finished. Put all that away. Sit on your hands if you need to, and let them turn the pages. Let them ask every question they want, and rather than answer them, play psychologist and turn the question back to them to answer. ("Why do you think the mommy bunny turned into the wind?") Turn it into a game: How far can your exploration take you? How long can you "read" and discuss one book?

Let one question lead to another and see where your conversation, where that narrative, leads. Then when you've finished the book, hand it to your child and ask them to tell you the story. It's eye opening to see what they're getting from each reading, compared with what we suppose they're getting.

Why This Matters

You are your child's first teacher—and young children learn best by example. Be the kind of reader you hope your child will be.

The best role models are in the home: moms and dads, brothers and sisters, grandmas and grandpas. If your child sees you reading, she will learn that reading is something you value. If he sees you reading voraciously—books, magazines, cereal boxes—he'll want to imitate that natural and valued behavior. An article on the Reading Is Fundamental website says it bluntly: "As much as they may deny it, most children want to be like their parents. Their lifelong habits start to form at the earliest ages, often by mimicking older members of the family. If they see you reading daily—both for function and for pleasure—they will more likely become avid readers themselves" (www.rif.org/).

Researchers in the last decade have discovered certain cells in the brain—mirror neurons—that fire not only when we perform an action, but when we watch someone else do so. This system of mirror neurons forms the basis for learning by imitation. Dr. Andrew Meltzoff, director of the Institute for Learning and Brain Sciences at the University of Washington, has published groundbreaking research on infants' natural interest—and abilities—in mirroring behavior. The institute has acquired the world's first scanner for babies' brains (dubbed the MEG). With MEG, a child is fitted with a sort of helmet that measures the magnetic field generated by neurons' electrical currents. Though the technology is new, early tests indicate reliability.

"Now we can begin to look at the origins and development of mirror neurons in human infants," Meltzoff says. "What happens when they look at their mother's face and watch her actions? Seeing images of how that is embodied in the baby's brain will be incredibly important in understanding early learning" (Slomski 2008).

These discoveries focus on how important role models are in early childhood for a range of learning skills and development. "Babies come into the world able to imitate and become members of their culture by observing what others do and incorporating those behaviors into their repertoire," says Meltzoff (Slomski 2008).

Meltzoff and his team have confirmed that when babies watch people reach for objects—or watch them doing activities, including reading—the same motor regions of the brain are activated in the babies as if they were doing the actions themselves. Even a child under 12 months of age learns about reading through imitation.

So, just by watching the people around them read a book, infants and young children are learning much more than we ever realized about the reading process.

Early reading can occur naturally and comfortably as part of language development.

There is a wealth of research on the importance of reading aloud to children. No doubt you've heard it before, but if you'd like resources, we'd recommend the position statement by the National Association for the Education of Young Children at www.naeyc.org/files/yc/file/200303/ReadingAloud.pdf.

Their summary includes the following statement: "The single most important activity for building these understandings and skills essential for reading success appears to be reading aloud to children (Wells 1985; Bus, Van Ijzendoorn, & Pellegrini 1995)."

It's also important to remember that reading to your child does not mean teaching her how to read. Follow his lead in creating stories, playing with print, and talking about illustrations. Brain researcher Jill Stamm concludes the following:

> *Nothing in neuroscience suggests that it's useful to hook a one-year-old on phonics or run alphabet drills with a two-year-old. In fact, there's little developmental advantage to learning to read before school. Some kids do and that's fine, but early reading is not linked to advanced performance later. Reading to a child, on the other hand, expands the total number of words your child hears, processes, and knows, which we now know to be critical to overall intelligence. Being read to also paves the way for skills involved in actual reading later.* (Stamm 2008, 241)

Children need regular and interactive experiences with books and print. When they see books in their environment, and are read to often, they learn that reading is valuable and enjoyable. And they pick up intangible book concepts without being taught—like the basic conventions of print: we read from left to right and top to bottom (in English and many other languages); there is a specific vocabulary about reading (words such as *page, letter, word, cover*). Children don't need to be "taught" these concepts; they need to experience them. The more you can make reading a natural part of life, the easier the task of becoming a reader will be.

CHAPTER 3

Media Matters

Fifty years ago this chapter wouldn't have existed. Ten years ago it would have been about a page long and would have just quoted the American Association of Pediatrics guidelines of no television for kids under two years old and limiting television watching to less than an hour a day for older kids. But today, you can't ignore that there are multiple forms of literacy, and that navigating our world, which is media rich and filled with various screens, means we have to consider carefully what that means when raising a "literate" child. Although vigorous and emotional discussions take place at preschools and playgrounds and online, it feels like we're all trying to find the balance between raising technologically illiterate Luddites who won't be able to find a job (or use a phone, listen to music, or perform the most basic functions in society) and obese couch potato zombies who can't read, have A.D.D., and grow up to live in our basements, hacking websites and playing video games.

The exciting and scary thing about how fast technology is changing is that there are no official guidelines. No one knows what reading on e-readers (perhaps like the one you have in your hand to read this book) will do to the eyesight and brain functions of kids two, five, or twenty years from now. We're all making it up as we go, and flying by the seat of our pants.

I think I'm a fairly good example of this dichotomy. I am a writer and I love to read. I still send handwritten notes for every occasion. I was raised in a house without a television until I was ten years old. Yet I went to film school. I love movies. I live in Hollywood, and my husband and most of our friends make their livings in film and (increasingly) television. I have worked in the Internet industry since its infancy. Our friends who don't work in entertainment work in the Web business. I do most of my shopping and business, and a decent chunk of my socializing, online. I love old and new media. And I want my kids to be fluent and literate in all the various forms of media and technology. So without doctor guidelines or historical data, I have worked (with my researcher mum and iPhone-addict husband) to come up with a "media literacy" approach that works for our family. I think that right now, there isn't a right answer, there's a "what's right *right now* for my family" answer. What follows in this chapter is some insight into the factors we considered and the thought process that went behind the approach we are following in our house regarding *media* literacy.

I Hate TV, but YouTube Is Another Matter

There is nothing more annoying than the self-righteous parent. In fact, I just read a pulpy mystery (I am completely addicted to them) in which a character's entire personality is summed up with the description that "she was one of those moms who loudly and proudly didn't let her children watch television." And this trait alone served as explanation for why her husband left her and why all the other characters sympathized with him.

I am always oddly embarrassed about admitting to other parents our own family rules that seem holier-than-thou. Until they were two, my kids didn't eat sugar (and then Halloween happened). When possible, we eat organic food. And finally, we don't watch television. I don't think television is evil, but I do think it's a slippery slope, so if they don't know about it, they can't want it.

We did institute family movie night. This began at about age two and a half where on Saturday nights we would all gather on the couch for a 15-minute episode of *Olivia*, followed by five minutes from *Bob Dylan Live at Newport* (have I mentioned that they're Bob Dylan obsessed?). Then we graduated to some *Marx Brothers, Singin' in the Rain*, and *Mary Poppins*. Watching maybe a half hour each movie night meant it would take us a month to get through a movie. Then when they turned four, we went to a movie in the theater, too, and now sometimes we watch as much as 45 minutes of a movie at a time on movie night (usually when it's a movie I really want to rewatch, like *The Princess Bride*).

Are you getting that we really don't watch much on our television at all? Because we don't. On the other hand, I don't want them to grow up so television-deprived that they have to pay kids five cents in kindergarten to tell them what happened on the *A-Team*. (But that's another story from my own television-deprived youth—thanks, Mom!)

What's all this leading up to? So far I sound completely like the quintessential smug and annoying PC mom. Here's my confession: we all LOVE YouTube. I have this conversation over and over with myself: is this different from television at all? It's sitting mesmerized by a little screen, after all, and my children probably sit closer to the computer or tablet than they would the television. I've thought about it a lot, and here's my (self-justifying) list of why YouTube is NOT TELEVISION, and is probably really very good for the kids.

1. They don't watch it alone; it's an activity we all do together. Yes, the same could be said for television, but I think there's a greater temptation to walk out of the room or read a magazine with television. But I can't leave them alone for more than thirty seconds with my computer, or Jacob will reconfigure it.

2. I pick exactly what they're exposed to. Again, you could do that with television by recording something and watching it and fast-forwarding through any commercials, but with YouTube, I watch each clip before they do, and there are no commercials.
3. There's some COOL SH*T on YouTube! Our early favorites were Feist singing "1-2-3-4" on *Sesame Street* and Maurice Sendak's Pierre from *Really Rosie*. No one I know remembers the cartoon *Barbapapa* except my brother and me. I finally got to show them what it's all about, and frankly, even though they didn't know it, it was an awesome bonding moment. Uncle Nathan even got the kids *Barbapapa* plates that they love. We also watch a lot of early *Smurfs* episodes. I can shower in the time it takes them to watch one, and then get dressed and put on makeup in the time it takes to watch the other twin's pick.
4. Finally, it's really easy to show them whatever we're all currently interested in. Obsessed with flamingos today? Molly and I looked up flamingo and watched those beautiful birds, without a trek to the zoo. When Jacob loved saying, "Is your mama a llama? Noooooooo" before bed, we looked up what real llamas look like. I was singing "Baa Baa Black Sheep" for a while, and we happened to see that they had a story clip of it—it turned out to be a cartoon from India, and the kids loved the accents. Not to mention, there are plenty of Bob Dylan clips, so we'll never run out.

Screen Time

One of the biggest problems parents face is setting limits. Kids want and need boundaries. How else can they test them? (And in the process, test our patience? Over and over and over again.) So we set up rules about food: how much sugar, how many treats, when and if to snack, and so on. We set up rules about sleep: when bedtime is, what the ritual is, and just how many more glasses of water, trips to the bathroom, or ice packs (that's the new one at our house, where every night someone manages to "get hurt" and desperately need an ice pack to soothe a boo-boo so they can get to sleep) are allowed. And in today's world, we need to set up rules about screen time.

Screens are everywhere, and it's no longer enough to set a Television Rule (be it none, only on weekends, one hour a day, or some variation thereof); you have to take into account *all* screen time. You can stick to your "no television" rule pretty strictly, and then realize that between computers, games, electronic tablets, smartphones, and even monitors in elevators and grocery stores, your kids have spent a couple of hours in front of a screen every day. Media, mixed media, is everywhere and bombards all of us in insidious ways without our consciousness even picking up on it.

One day we walked by a bus stop on the way to the park with my friend and her son, who, like Molly and Jacob, was three years old. There was a huge poster of whatever kids' movie was popular at the time, perhaps *Tangled*. All three kids ran over to it. Molly and Jacob stared up, openmouthed. But their friend ran right to it and began pushing his hands across the ad. My face must have reflected the question in my head ("What the hell is he doing?"), because my friend started to laugh. "He's trying to turn the page," she said. "He loves our iPad so much, he thinks everything is a touch screen. He does this to magazines and even books sometimes."

I was equal parts impressed and horrified. I hadn't let Molly and Jacob play with an iPad, iPhone, or e-book yet. To be honest, I'm not sure if it was just because I didn't have one for myself or because I was opposed to it. This three-year-old's actions seemed advanced, but also a little sad—he didn't realize that books had pages to turn, not swipe. That evening, my husband and I sat down to talk screen strategy. We definitely don't want our kids to be the ones who can't eat in a restaurant without playing Angry Birds on the phone, yet we also don't want Luddites who can't function in society or get jobs. Screen literacy is a type of literacy, too. What to do?

Our Rules

Here are the basics:

1. Television is for "movies" only, and the only (non-caveated) time to watch a movie is on the weekly "movie night." In our house, this is Saturday. Movie night does not last more than an hour (it was half an hour until the twins were four years old), again, unless it's an exceptional reason.
2. Movie theaters are a special treat. We probably go three times a year. I'm not sure if this is because we want to limit their exposure, or because most kids' movies are garbage that we can't force ourselves to sit through, or because it's too expensive to take a family of four more often than that.
3. Video games are a "no." Period. I'm sure this will get revisited as they get older. But so far they aren't asking for them, and we're not telling about them.
4. We treat computer games the same way we treat YouTube. We have introduced only a few—mainly *Sesame Street* and a couple of car or puzzle games.
5. Computer videos, aka YouTube (at our house). This is our big daily screen time. It's my shower time—I get to shower and get dressed, they get to curl up on our bed with my laptop and pick a few clips on YouTube. When we started this, we were much more strict than we are now—I'd find vintage Beatles or Bob Dylan performances or clips from musicals. I quickly realized that they were clicking around from there and finding loud or inappropriate "related" clips that would have them

howling and me rushing, dripping wet, out of the shower. In desperation, I introduced them to *The Smurfs* cartoons from my own childhood. An 11-minute episode got me through the shower, and the second episode let me get dressed, slap makeup on, and get my coffee. So we started as a 22-minute-a-day family, but have since tacked on a third episode (which lets me actually drink my coffee). Is it ideal? Probably not. Am I a better mom when I'm clean and caffeinated? Definitely. So there we are.
6. iPhones—only Mommy and Daddy touch these. If we're desperate (waiting in a doctor's office with a sick kid), we show them fun apps, games, or clips, but they're not allowed to hold the phone. We both rely on the phone too much for work stuff to let one of them reprogram our lifelines.
7. E-readers/Tablets—We have them, but the kids don't. They are allowed to use them for reading books only, and only when they are being forced to wait for their sibling. So when Molly is at ballet class, Jacob can read books on my Kindle. When Jacob has his golf lesson, Molly can use it (though she chooses not to—she prefers real books or telling stories).

Our rules aren't perfect and they're always changing, but they work for us right now. Check back with us next year, when the kids are in first grade and each child is assigned an iPad with voice recognition software to do their homework, and it may be a different story. (I initially wrote that as a joke, but there are now several second grades in our city that assign each child an iPad for the year. That's how fast technology changes, and probably how fast our family rules will change too!)

Have you thought about your family rules? Just like having an emergency escape plan, it's good to have a media consumption plan that both parents have signed off on. You might wish to initiate a discussion with your parenting partners (spouse, partner, parent, child care provider) about your house rules for media consumption. It's interesting to have this discussion, because you may have one set of rules in your head, and the person or people you parent with may have a whole different set. Or it may even be something that you've never thought about but have done instinctively. Once you've discussed your guidelines, try the following exercise:

1. Write down your family guidelines.
2. Track your screen time for a week—your child's and your own (don't forget to include the time you spend at work on the computer, texting or checking maps on your smartphone, or reading on your tablet or e-reader . . . It's all screen time!)
3. How closely does your child's actual screen time match up with their "allotted" amount?
4. Now, how about your own?

The point of this exercise is to acknowledge how much time we as a society spend in front of screens. It's not necessarily good or bad—it's a form of literacy, too. But even though many of us have hard-and-fast television rules (for our children, and maybe even for ourselves), it's rather shocking to realize how much time we spend in front of screens.

What About Apps?

Speaking of iPads (and other tablets) . . . I started to write a section on fabulous book apps, just like I would write a section on a particular type of book recommendations. Then I stopped, and decided to write this explanation for the lack of recommendations instead, because there really aren't any apps I let the kids play with. I'd have to research which ones are cool and I like, and then I still wouldn't use them with the kids. I'd just be recommending the ones I would use if I were going to use them. I'm not an expert in what I don't use, so that felt disingenuous.

Are there some ridiculously fantastic apps for tablets and smartphones for kids' books (like *The Fantastic Flying Books of Mr. Morris Lessmore*, which is so cool I can hardly stand it)? Definitely! But for me, it's too slippery a slope. It's far too easy for me to turn handing them the iPad with a book app to keep them busy into watching a movie just this once, and then a movie every day. I'm not against it in general; I'm against it for my family.

Also, I figure it's like chocolate cake. Utterly wonderful? Yep! But my job as a parent is to make sure they love vegetables and fruits and fish and other healthy, vitamin-laden, good-for-you yumminess. I have no doubt that they'll discover chocolate (or technology) with time—that they'll adore it and go through spurts of consuming nothing else. But if I've done my job as a parent, ideally the foundation of love for the truly great stuff (be it brussels sprouts, Shakespeare, or the Beatles) is underneath a love of chocolate cake, book apps, and Auto-Tune sounds.

Why This Matters

Children are growing up in an electronic world. Families can establish reasonable guidelines for electronic-media use that help their children grow up in an ever-changing media climate.

Electronic media: We all have our history and our relationship with it—and most parents of young children wonder about its influence on their kids. Many mothers and fathers struggle to understand the role screen time can have in our children's lives: how much, which programs, and what is educational about "educational media." Luckily for us, there are resources to help guide us in making informed choices. Lisa Guernsey (2007) dug into current research in child development, interviewed people who are studying the effects of different programming on children below the age of five, and came up with fascinating and helpful information, which she put in her book *Into the Minds of Babes: How Screen Time Affects Young Children from Birth to Age Five*.

For example, the American Association of Pediatrics (AAP) recommends no television—or screen time—at all before the age of two. Guernsey learned that the AAP had no research basis for such an extreme mandate, and that there really are positive aspects of television and screen time for very young children. But she also discovered how play and language development are negatively affected by the background noise of television, and what programs might—and might not—be age appropriate for your child. Her conclusions are highlighted by thoughtful, reader-friendly advice in each chapter. It's a great resource.

Her categories for how families make informed choices gives a very helpful framework for how to take into account content, context, and the needs of their children. She urges families to consider the following:

1. Instituting time limits
2. Creating rules about when to turn the television on
3. Controlling the content their children can watch
4. Limiting exposure to commercials and big-business marketing
5. Limiting background TV
6. Integrating other forms of electronic media into their lives
7. Discussing ways to cope with multiple children of different ages

These categories are a starting point, and help families discuss their unique needs and the needs of each child. What is frightening or overstimulating for one child will be an exciting adventure for another. Watching a program with your child may make it possible to explain the content of an educational program that would be inappropriate for her to watch alone. Guernsey has formulated wise strategies for focusing on what she calls the three Cs: content, context, and the individual child. Keeping these three Cs in mind, parents can create the best set of guidelines for their own family.

> Even interactive screen time is still much less active than "live."

Some other research to keep in mind: new studies have shown that children learn better from live people than they do from people on a screen (Rideout, Vanderwater, and Wartella 2003). Researcher Patricia Kuhl (codirector of the Institute for Learning and Brain Sciences at the University of Washington) believes it is the *shared eye-gazing* that takes place in live interaction that helps the brain process information differently (Dewar 2009).

One of the AAP suggestions that gets less attention is a great one: use television and screen time to weave a "web of learning" for your child. For example, look for library books related to characters or subjects in the programs you see. You might talk about them when the television is off. There are many activities you can do at home that mimic or complement those seen on TV, such as taking a nature walk, finger painting, or building a particular scene or your own imaginary world out of blocks. Once you start brainstorming, you'll find that the options are limitless—and because you are creating them, they will be perfectly tailored to your child's needs.

PART TWO

What to Read

Now you've got the house set up, all ready to read to your little one. But what exactly should you read? Everyone has the list of books they remember fondly from childhood, the list of classics firmly implanted in their brains, and the "starter set" that almost everyone gets at their baby shower: *Pat the Bunny* (Kunhardt 1940), *Goodnight Moon* (Brown 1947), *Guess How Much I Love You* (McBratney 1994), and at least a Seuss or two. Then what? You tear through (and tire of) those pretty fast. Your baby is calling out for stimulation, and your sleep-deprived brain can't begin to think of what to read.

The short answer is read anything, read everything, and read what engages you. And pretty soon, faster than you can imagine when they're so little, your kids will begin telling you what they like. But just in case you'd like a few suggestions to get you going, or to supplement the library you are already creating at home, I thought I'd give you some ideas that worked for us.

CHAPTER 4

ABCs

"Let's start at the very beginning. A very good place to start. When you read you begin with A-B-C . . ."
—Maria, from *The Sound of Music*

The ABCs *are* a good place to start, because alphabet books contain so much more than just the alphabet. There are alphabet books for big kids, alphabets as a way to teach things, and alphabets as an entry into other languages (and worlds). So start with the alphabet for the youngest of babies, but also branch out and get some slightly more sophisticated ABC books for your kids to grow into. You may be surprised at how much they (and you!) continue to get from these books.

First Alphabet Books

For babies and toddlers, the key to finding a book that will hold their interest is choosing one they can interact with in some way. For alphabet books, this could mean guessing letters or sounds, enjoying vibrant colors, or relating to favorite objects and activities. These were some of our favorite first alphabet books:

ABC: A Child's First Alphabet Book by Alison Jay

Like the title says, this is the perfect first alphabet book for any child. The beautifully illustrated text invites a young reader to enjoy the pictures and match the sounds of the letters to many objects on a page. The images are familiar objects that toddlers will easily recognize and appreciate exploring. There is also a subtle underlying story that weaves the pages together.

The Turn-Around, Upside-Down Alphabet Book by Lisa Campbell Ernst

This inventive alphabet book invites children (and adults) to explore each letter in four ways. Each time you turn the letter, it becomes a different object. For example, when *J* is rotated clockwise, it becomes, in turn, an elephant's trunk, a candy cane, and a monkey's tail. With a young child, you can point out the letters and enjoy the bold graphics. But this is also a book that can grow with the child, reexploring to understand how the author has played with the letters. As we discussed earlier, playing with letters (be they in block, foam, magnet, or food form) is a powerful way for kids to learn. It's great to teach them that books are for playing with, too!

Q Is for Duck: An Alphabet Guessing Game by Mary Elting and Michael Folsom illustrated by Jack Kent

This one is a great variation from the standard alphabet book. Here, the letter doesn't stand for the object, but for the sound it makes. Even very young children can figure out most of these riddles, and they love to make the animal sounds. It's a hit as an interactive book—and of course, you can make up other words to match the various letters with the more "expected" animal or object.

The Alphabet Room by Sara Pinto

Children get to interact with this alphabet book in a different way—by lifting the flaps. Books like this were early favorites of

Molly and Jacob, and remain so to this day. Each letter has a door to a warm yellow room, which fills with objects as you progress through the book. There is a gentle humor to the inviting pictures that adults as well as young children can enjoy together. It's also fun to continue to search for items on the pages, learning new objects and names with each rereading.

Alphabeep!: A Zipping, Zooming ABC by Debora Pearson, illustrated by Edward Miller

This one is for the kid who loves everything about trucks and cars and machines on the road. The brightly illustrated alphabet book is packed with vehicles and people in action. Young children love learning new words like *zamboni* as well as recognizing their favorites like *vans* and *tractors*. An added bonus is the list of websites for downloading upper- and lowercase letters as well as road signs and truck cutouts. You can find alphabet books on almost every subject, and finding one that appeals to something basic that your child adores (such as cars and trucks) can be a great way to keep them turning the pages.

Alphabet Books for Big Kids

When Molly and Jacob were tiny toddlers, I got frustrated with many alphabet books, including some of our favorites. With the myopia that is characteristic of new parents, all I could think of was the particular way my own kids were interacting with a book or toy. The problem with these books? Many of them used lowercase letters. They made me crazy. They confused the kids to no end, and made me endure what felt like hours of this circular talk: "That's an *A*. No, I know it doesn't look like one, but it's a different kind of *A*. It's called lowercase. Yes, it is. And that's an *A*, too. Okay, you're right. Only that big one is an *A*. I don't know what that letter is called. It must be a new one they invented since I was little. Yes, I'll find out what it is. Yes, I'll ask Daddy. That's a great idea."

What were those idiot authors and illustrators and publishers thinking? All alphabet books should have only uppercase letters. Alphabet books are for little kids!

Well, I was wrong on two counts. First of all, by age four both my kids not only knew both uppercase and lowercase letters, but loved writing with both and recognizing both. Molly had even made up her own "case"—the "curlycase." Young kids *do* like letters in all their various cases, fonts, and forms, and with repeated exposure, they learn to recognize all of them.

Second, what was I thinking when I assumed that alphabet books were only for kids first learning the alphabet? Even as Molly and Jacob began to read books all by themselves, they still loved alphabet books. Why shouldn't they? *I* still love alphabet books. Alphabet books can challenge the way you think of using letters, they can tell a story, and they can even make you look at things in a different way. After your kids have graduated from those fabulous first alphabet books, here are some books that will grow *with* kids, and grow *on* you. (Hardbound alphabet books actually make great gifts for teens and adults, if you're ever looking for a unique present. I often give Mary Azarian's *A Farmer's Alphabet* [1981] as a housewarming gift because the illustrations look gorgeous framed and hanging in a new kitchen or pantry.)

> *Peanut Butter and Jellyfishes: A Very Silly Alphabet Book* by
> Brian P. Cleary, illustrated by Betsy E. Snyder

Each letter of the alphabet is hidden in the illustrations of this alphabet book. The word pictures of sentences are as wacky as the bright and colorful collages: *K* has kilt-wearing kittens, as well as kangaroos kissing. There are details to pore over, and a kind of "Where's Waldo?" compulsion to find all 10 *N*s or 6 *Z*s, as listed on the end pages. Another plus: the printing is big and bright, easy to read and recognize, and the verses are lots of fun.

The Sweet and Sour Animal Book by Langston Hughes, illustrated by the students from the Harlem School of the Arts

Twenty-six recently discovered alphabet animal poems by poet Langston Hughes are illustrated by the 3-D art of young children in Harlem. Full-color photographs of the artwork illustrate each gem of a poem. Hughes's alphabet poems have his signature wit and imagination. This is definitely a book that may take time for kids to learn to love. I fell in love with it and bought it for Molly and Jacob, thinking that they'd love Hughes's words and the cool illustrations that other kids had made. Molly promptly burst into tears (this was at age three) and brought the book to my room, saying it was too scary and that she couldn't sleep when it was in her room. Looking at it with that thought in mind, I realized the young artists had created characters with a decidedly Tim Burton "off and odd" air. The book remained tucked under my mattress for about a year, when I reintroduced it. Now both kids really like it—the verse and the illustrative creations have inspired several arts and crafts sessions at home.

The Alphabet Tree by Leo Lionni

Leo Lionni's alphabet book is a brilliant metaphorical story of the power of the word in a democratic society, as the word-bug and the purple caterpillar teach the letters of the alphabet how they can be stronger when they work together and create words, then whole sentences. This theme might not be what your toddler responds to, at least not yet. But that subtle message makes it more appealing for adults, and gives you something to think about (and subtly indoctrinate your kids with) as you read the book for the 20th time in a row (which your kids will insist on). The notion of the Alphabet Tree is also a terrific teaching tool as young children begin to solve the written language puzzle.

Alligators All Around: An Alphabet by Maurice Sendak

Who wouldn't love an alphabet book with pages like *N* for Never Napping or *P* for Pushing People, all illustrated with endearing and personality-filled alligators? Sendak's voice is immediately recognizable, reminding readers of *Where the Wild Things Are* (1963) as the alligators strut across the pages. The words are also set to music in a song in *Really Rosie*, a musical written by Sendak (1986), with music by Carole King.

> *Alphabeasties: And Other Amazing Types* by Sharon Werner and Sarah Forss

This alphabet book is another of the ones that delights parents as well as kids, and although preschoolers love it, older kids who are quite familiar with the ins and outs of the alphabet adore it as well. On the surface, it's a cute alphabet book that makes an animal for each letter, composed of that letter. But on deeper inspection, there's more. It's also a love letter to fonts and typography, showing how a simple font choice can inform how we feel about the words presented. (A bat made up of gothic *b*s makes you think that it will turn into a vampire, elongated *g*s emphasize the giraffe's height, and so forth.) It's an interesting introduction to both the alphabet and to the notion that not only can words make art in the form of books, but sometimes the words themselves are art.

Many Languages, Many Alphabets

I've already talked about the variety of alphabet blocks in different languages we have for the kids to play with. And although none of us in the family is bilingual, we all love languages and have studied them in the past. It makes me sad that I can't speak another language with enough fluency to have the kids grow up in a bilingual household (that's a topic for another book), but we do love to play with languages. Molly in particular loves the sounds that other languages make. I try to encourage and extend this love of foreign words and sounds to our favorite media: books. Luckily, Ruth (my expert mum) has done tons of research in multilingual classrooms and with kids who are English language learners, so I asked her for some alphabet book recommendations that showcase different alphabets in other languages. From the list she came up with, these are the ones that quickly became favorites in our house:

My First Arabic Alphabet Book by Siddiqa Juma

This beautiful little Arabic alphabet book has everything a successful picture book for young children should: clear, inviting pictures; large print that encourages little fingers to trace; and sturdy board-book construction. Because Arabic writing is read right-to-left, the book is bound intentionally to accommodate babies learning to turn pages authentically for the Arabic language.

Azbooka—Russian ABC's—in Russian Language by Tatiana Bokova

Russian children and their friends and classmates will appreciate the chance to see the letters of the Cyrillic alphabet displayed on each page, along with Russian words that begin each letter sound. Kids like the bold primary colors and familiar images alongside a different set of symbols. (See photo 4-1.)

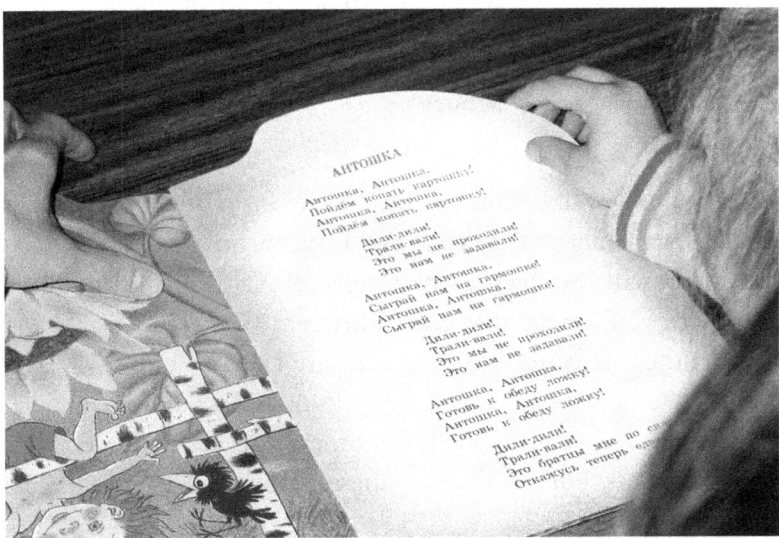

Photo 4-1: This book features the Cyrillic alphabet.

Just in Case: A Trickster Tale and Spanish Alphabet Book by Yuyi Morales

Grandma Beetle is having a birthday party. What should Señor Calvera bring? With help from a ghostly guide, Señor Calvera chooses from an array of items, trying to decide what Grandma Beetle would love the most. This amusing and original alphabet tale celebrates the Day of the Dead, with Señor Calvera as one of the skeleton party guests. There is whimsy and enchantment galore along with pictures that invite repeated readings.

Alef-Bet: A Hebrew Alphabet Book by Michelle Edwards

The oil-pastel illustrations are the highlight of this Hebrew alphabet book. Readers see the letters of the alphabet, words beginning with each, and their English translations, all in the context of the activities of a creative, busy, and loving family. Bathtub splashing, pillow fights, and different seasonal activities encourage young readers to make connections between their daily experiences and the family in the picture book.

If your kids are as fascinated as mine were (and are) at first encountering "other alphabets" (as Molly and Jacob call non-Western letters), they may want to see more of the languages than just the ABCs. These are some of our favorite books that continue the exploration of other languages:

At the Beach by Huy Voun Lee

As Xiao Ming walks along the beach with his mother, she teaches him several Chinese characters and explains how they show what they represent. Readers learn along with Xiao Ming in this first of a series of books that teach different Chinese symbols and explain their derivation. Equally fine are Lee's other books *In the Park* (1998) and *In the Snow* (2000). (Note: Mandarin pronunciation guides are also provided. Cantonese speakers will recognize the characters but pronounce them differently from the text guides.)

Waiting for Mama by Tae-Joon Lee, illustrated by
Dong-Sung Kim

This simple story is a universal tale: a little boy is waiting for his mother. He tries to wait patiently, but keeps asking for her as the sun begins to go down and she still has not arrived. This picture book is special for its setting at a Korean train station and was originally published in a newspaper in 1938. The pastel-and-ink illustrations go beautifully with the sweet story; I especially love the picture on the last page of the mother and child walking hand in hand through a snow-covered village. The Korean text is also translated into English, making the book accessible to a wide audience.

My Name Is Yoon by Helen Recorvits, illustrated by
Gabi Swiatkowska

Yoon is the narrator of this story of a young Korean immigrant. Yoon's name means "shining wisdom," and when she writes it in Korean, it looks happy, "like dancing figures." Her father teaches her to write *Yoon* in English, and she is not pleased with the way it looks on the page, even though her father stresses that it still means "shining wisdom." Though there is little Korean writing in the text, the book does a good job of exploring Yoon's mixed emotions about the differences in writing in two different languages.

The Magic Pocket by Michio Mado, illustrated by
Mitsumasa Anno, translated by the Empress Michiko of
Japan. In English and Japanese

This lovely book filled with bright pictures is sparely presented yet compelling. Simple images convey childhood experiences such as breaking a cookie in your pocket, walking under an umbrella, or listening to the sounds of musical instruments. Both the original Japanese and the English translations are included.

Why This Matters

Memorizing the alphabet is not nearly as important as just being familiar with letters and playing creatively with the sounds they represent.

Symbols, letters, words, and print messages surround babies, toddlers, and young children. The more familiarity they have with how print, like words, can communicate ideas and stories, the more comfortable they will be as young readers and writers. Providing natural and fun experiences with letters and sounds helps children understand the *alphabetic principle* and make the letter-sound connections that are so necessary to becoming successful readers and writers. (The *alphabetic principle* refers to an understanding that there is a systematic relationship between letters and sounds.) The National Research Council recommends that we help children enjoy and appreciate the *beauty* of the alphabet (Burns, Griffin, and Snow 1999). Alphabet books and playing with letters and shapes helps children see the differences among the different letters, helping make learning easier, too.

You may hear teachers talk about phonemic awareness as a key ingredient in learning to read and write. Phonemic awareness refers to a child's understanding that speech is made up of "identifiable units" such as spoken words, syllables, and sounds. Children who are "phonemically aware" can think about and manipulate sounds in words. The roots of that awareness of sound are best found in nursery rhymes and rhyming games—and in many of the alphabet books that play with sound in creative and entertaining ways. It's easy and fun, natural and playful, to encourage this skill without trying to teach it, or "drill and kill" it. Many studies show that even older children acquire phonemic awareness without specific training as a consequence of learning to read (Wagner and Torgensen 1987; Ehri 1994). The best recommendation: informally learning letters and sounds, words, and rhyming through great picture books, including the fantastic alphabet books that abound.

Children who are emergent bilingual learners (often called English language learners) are more likely to learn English if they are already familiar with reading and writing concepts and ideas in their first language—including written language through alphabet books and alphabet blocks—and even pictograph and logograph symbol systems such as Japanese, Korean, and Chinese. Providing non-English materials and resources to all kids helps them appreciate the wonder of worldwide languages. Children are fascinated by the brushstrokes that represent whole words, for example, and can appreciate the literacy of cultures other than their own. It's a natural first step in helping our kids know they are world citizens!

CHAPTER 5

123s

A lot of my friends have phobias about math. When I ask them why, they're inevitably thinking about an isolated geometry or algebra class in high school, not the concept of the beauty of math in our everyday world. I love math. I want Molly and Jacob to love it, too, and to think of it as something that is part of everything we do—part of every project and problem, artistic creation, or musical endeavor. As I've been teaching the kids about the 1-2-3 counterpart to A-B-C, I want them to see it as fun and as much a part of everything as a color or a word might be. That is the through line with all the number books listed below—they all roll math into something beautiful and useful and make it a part of other thoughts and discussions and ideas.

Great Counting Books

Before you get to advanced math, you learn to count: 1-2-3. These were our favorite first counting books. They all tell a story, make you laugh, make you think, and make you look a little differently at the world and at numbers.

One Child, One Seed: A South African Counting Book by Kathryn Cave, photographs by Gisele Wulfsohn

More than a counting book, *One Child, One Seed* is also a fascinating exploration of South African community living. The beautiful photographs are artistically arranged on the pages to help tell the story of a seed's life, and also entice readers with intriguing counting opportunities. Details of everyday life are woven into the story as we have the chance to explore the games, transportation, rituals, and home culture of the village. We are even provided with a recipe for *isijingi*, the pumpkin stew that is eaten at the traditional harvest feast. (We are big fans of anything with a recipe, and this makes for a fun companion piece to *Pumpkin Soup* [Cooper 2009], one of Molly and Jacob's favorite books from age two.) Simple rhyming text makes this universal story a great read-aloud.

Two of Everything: A Chinese Folktale by Lily Toy Hong

Both humorous and wise, this folktale tells the story of a magic pot that doubles whatever is placed in it. Discovered by a poor farmer, it seems to be a great gift for him and his wife, who duplicate coin purses and enough gold to fill their hut. But their fortune changes again when they fall into the pot—and create their own doubles! How will they come to a successful resolution of their new life situation? With quick thinking, and lots of humor thrown in. Beautiful illustrations, mostly in greens and blues, are simple and clear—very fitting for the folktale genre. And the roly-poly people are just plain charming.

I Spy Two Eyes: Numbers in Art by Lucy Micklethwait

Is this a book of art appreciation—or a counting book? Happily, it's both! On the left-hand page are the numbers (written both as words and symbols) and an object to count, and on the right-hand page is a fine-art painting reproduction so the reader can find the object and count each one. Kids really enjoy hunting for the items in the pictures—and it's a great way for them to closely explore the art. The pictures represent a range of artistic styles and are well displayed and reproduced.

Ten Sly Piranhas by William Wise, illustrated by Victoria Chess

This counting-backward book is a terrific read-aloud, with its enticing rhyme and rhythm. It's a clever and humorous story about a group of devious fish—pink piranhas—who "with a gulp and a gurgle" devour one another . . . until there is one last piranha left. He, too, meets his fate when a crocodile enters "and then there were none." The watercolor and pen-and-ink illustrations are a treat, as they depict the river jungle environment and lots of critters, including turtles, snakes, toucans, and frogs.

City by Numbers by Stephen T. Johnson

This picture book features realistic paintings of an urban cityscape. Numbers are hidden throughout the paintings, but you have to look closely at the architecture to find them. For example, the number *8* is created by two trash-can rims side by side. It's a wonderfully creative and artistic book that adults will enjoy for the fascinating architectural detail and beautifully rendered drawings.

Beyond Counting: Math Picture Books

Good picture books are a great way to open mathematical discussions with children. There are quite a few excellent ones that correlate with mathematical topics, such as counting, beginning division, multiplication, and even the notion of zero. Our favorites (mine and the kids' alike) are those that also feature engaging stories, inviting language, and high-quality illustrations. Here are a few to introduce to your young learners as you explore all kinds of math concepts—and relish the pleasures of good books at the same time.

A Place for Zero: A Math Adventure by
Angeline Sparagna Lopresti and Phyllis Hornung

It's fun to introduce the properties of zero to early readers in a story format. Poor zero! He feels sad and left out among the other digits. In the course of the tale, he meets intriguing mathematical characters such as Count Infinity, and readers are introduced to all the ways we rely on the concept of nothing—and its role in place value, infinity, and numerical operations overall. Although some concepts will be beyond the youngest readers, it's still a wonderful preview of mathematical adventures to come. The illustrations are bright and appealing, too.

Each Orange Had 8 Slices by Paul Giganti, illustrated by
Donald Crews

Bright and fun illustrations are the greatest draw of this book. But this vibrant little book is more than beautiful; it's also a wonderful introduction to mathematical thinking. Patterning, multiplication, and creative problem solving are all within its pages in addition to counting, which makes it a wonderful book for multiage classrooms as well as families with children of different ages or mathematical interests or abilities. There's something mathematical for kids from kindergarten through about grade 3—and the gorgeous illustrations are for all ages.

The Coin Counting Book by Rozanne Lanczak Williams

Coins are a tangible, hands-on, and enjoyable way to explore the concept of money—as well as mathematical ideas such as grouping, counting, and creating equivalent values. The photographs are clear and accessible, so children can pore over them. The simple rhymes are engaging, too. The book itself is large and easy to handle, making it ideal for young children to explore. It's also fun for kids who are just getting the idea of what money is and how it works in the world to be able to play with piles of real coins alongside the ones that live in the book.

Chapter 5

A Remainder of One by Elinor J. Pinczes, illustrated by Bonnie MacKain

Twenty-five beetles are on parade in this rhyming picture book, which also serves as a fine introduction to the concept of division. The blue bug queen "likes to keep things tidy," so she approves the two-by-two formation of the parade . . . except when she sees one is left over! This last bug, Joe, ends up being a "remainder," and to solve his dilemma, he tries out various formations: by threes, by fours, and finally one that works for him—by fives. The bugs are big, blue, and friendly looking, though each is unique.

365 Penguins by Jean-Luc Fromental, illustrated by Joëlle Jolivet

This lively and funny French import brings its own unique feel in both art and writing. Penguins start arriving, one a day, for a full year. How does the family deal with this penguin onslaught? Over the year, as penguins run amok in the house, the father decides to organize them—in boxes, by dozens, and even in cubic formation. The art is stunning, with comical birds shown in large, bright illustrations. There's an important ecological lesson, too, taught by the children's scientist Uncle Victor. Besides the fascinating mathematical problem solving, the book has a fun—and funny—narrative line. Kids too young to really "get" the math still love to search for Little Chilly—with his vibrant blue feet—on each page, and you'll be amazed after a year or so of having this on the shelf how many mathematical concepts they have accidentally absorbed.

Zero by Kathryn Otoshi

Both *Zero* and *One* (its award-winning predecessor) are about more than just numbers: they're about being who or what you are. *One* is about bullying and standing up for who you are and what you want to be—and it teaches kids that you can make a difference because "sometimes it just takes one." Molly and Jacob do like that book, but the clear favorite of the two books is *Zero*. This book is a clever wordplay on feeling like nothing and trying to be what you're not, and the difference between feeling like you "have a hole" and that you "are whole." It also sends the message that everyone has value and everyone can and does count. Sometimes, you just have to find out how. Numbers and self-esteem collide here, and kids are so entertained by the bouncy, bright numbers that they don't realize they're learning a couple of valuable lessons.

Math for the Whole Family: Read-Alouds

Most of us don't use advanced math every day. For many of us, that means that when we have to help our kids with math, we have to relearn it ourselves. Why wait till they're in calculus? Start brushing up on some math theory now!

These books are wonderful family read-alouds: they hold the interest of a wide age range as they beautifully illustrate either a mathematical principle or a way to see the world by using math.

All of these books feature math in a different way—some as puzzles, some as metaphors, some as ways of seeing life and its problems or the world in general. When you read these books, you'll start to see math everywhere—and even like it! That's actually why I wanted to include these books (besides the fact that I really love them). When I read them, they made me excited about math again, and they have helped me pass that excitement on to the kids. We play dorky math games in the car all the time, and they think math games with Mom are as fun as magic tricks with Dad. I think (or at least fervently hope) that this excitement will stay with them as they learn formal math lessons in school. I know it's made me dread helping them with advanced math homework a little less.

Blockhead: The Life of Fibonacci by Joseph D'Agnese, illustrated by John O'Brien

Although this is definitely a book for kids, with simple text and beautiful illustrations, it is a great read-aloud for everyone, regardless of the age of the youngest member of the family. When we discovered this book at the library, everyone in the family laid claim to it at some point, from four-year-olds to grandparents. Telling the story of Leonardo Fibonacci, the book illustrates many things to love about math, discovery, and the amazing way children (and adults who continue to explore like children) think. Called a blockhead by his teacher for always daydreaming, Leonardo continued to look at the world in his own way, discovering numbers and repetition and sequences everywhere. This is the clearest and most interesting description of the Fibonacci sequence I've seen, and will have everyone in the family understanding and looking at the world in a slightly different way.

Grandfather Counts by Andrea Cheng

Counting books are a natural starting point for math ideas with toddlers, and this one is a favorite. Counting in Chinese becomes the bridge between Helen and her Chinese grandfather Gong Gong as they watch trains and count the cars in both languages. Besides numbers, Helen and Gong Gong learn language, culture, and stories, and form a special bond, teaching each other in this powerful intergenerational story with math at its heart.

Minnie's Diner: A Multiplying Menu by Dayle Ann Dodds

A fun look at another math topic—exponentials. Papa McFay says no food till the work is done, but one by one his boys are tempted away from their chores by the delicious smells coming from Minnie's Diner. Each son is twice the size of the last, and proceeds to order twice as much food as the previous brother. It's fun for kids (and a cool visual reminder for adults) to see how fast things add up when you double them, as one cherry pie quickly becomes a teetering pile of 32 pies. Papa McFay comes in last, and judging by the gigantic shadow he casts, he should have no problem eating a double order, right? In any case, the book ends with a wiped-out, cleaned-out Minnie hanging a "Sorry, we're closed" sign!

Mummy Math: An Adventure in Geometry by
Cindy Neuschwander, illustrated by Bryan Langdo

How about an engaging story to introduce the concept of geometry? An adventure where you need to escape from a hidden pyramid is pretty enticing for exploring shapes. The twin brothers in the Zills family get stuck inside a pyramid with their dog and must use math to figure out a way to get out. The illustrations are well done and the story line is engaging. It's always a treat for the youngest readers to be in on the fun of seeking out hidden shapes in each picture.

Math Curse by Jon Scieszka, illustrated by Lane Smith

When Mrs. Fibonacci (!) tells her class that they can "think of almost everything as a math problem," one of the girls is instantly afflicted with a "math curse" where that's exactly what happens. With the silliness and cleverness that you expect from Scieszka and Smith, this book delights as it really does make you think about how many times and in how many ways we reference numbers every day.

You Can Count on Monsters by Richard Evan Schwartz

I love this book. Even when they were four and a half years old, the twins loved this book. My husband who tutored calculus throughout college and is really good at higher math loves this book. You will love this book. Beginning with an explanation of multiplication, prime numbers, composites, and factorization that will lose your average 4-year-old (or possibly even your 10-year-old) but will refresh adults, it turns into an art project that shows each number (1–100) as a monster made up of its prime composites. A factor tree and dot groupings on one side of the page show how a number is broken down into its smallest factors, and then those numbers are each represented as a monster that somehow incorporates that number into its being. So the monster of 27 is illustrated by three 3 monsters (triangle heads denote their "three-ness") cavorting together. Part art, part visual poetry, all math. If you're not someone who sees the world in numbers, or the beautiful patterns in math, this will help you begin to think that way.

The Number Devil: A Mathematical Adventure by
Hans Magnus Enzensberger

For many of us, dreaming of math and numbers would be more of a nightmare . . . and so it begins for Robert, who is visited in his dreams by the Number Devil. But soon he is searching for the Number Devil as soon as he falls asleep, as the devil explains how fascinating numbers are, and how they relate. Prime numbers become "prima donnas" and a factoral is called a "vroom!" and the patterns in math will simultaneously open your eyes and make your head spin, as they do for Robert. The book is told as a series of nights of sleep, with visits from the Number Devil, who explains increasingly difficult concepts. The first few dreams are easy and fun for everyone, and by the end of the book, it takes a few reads for any nonmathematicians to catch the drift, but this is a book that you can go to again and again for years of family read-alouds.

Everyday Math and Literacy

There are lots of ways to talk about math with your kids every day, no matter how old or young they are. Books about concepts are a great starting point from which to comfortably learn the way literacy helps us learn new ideas; in terms of number symbols and concepts, books can lead to more math adventures. "Everyday math" book extensions enrich those book concepts and deepen the rereadings.

I was thinking about how much we do it in our house—partially because I'm a math geek (my dad and I used to use an egg timer and race each other at doing logic problems—we're talking preteen years here—yikes!) and partially because it seems like everything we do lends itself to a discussion about math. But I was realizing that it's not just the favorite activities, it's the un-fun ones, too. As Mary Poppins says, "In every job that must be done, there is an element of fun. You find the fun and snap—the job's a game . . ."

So I thought I'd share how math crops up in *our* favorite and least favorite activities.

My favorite: Cooking is FULL of math. I may have mentioned one or a dozen times that I like to cook. Because I have to feed four people at least three times a day and keep everyone happy (this is sounding like a logic puzzle already), there is plenty of cooking to be done. Since the day the kids were born, they've been with me in the kitchen. It started with me pretending I had my own cooking show and talking to them about what I was doing, counting the ingredients as I cooked. Then we moved on to them helping by about age two, dumping and stirring, measuring and counting on their own. And when they hit four, we entered a whole new world of fun things to talk about in the kitchen: fractions. Sometimes it's with measuring cups, sometimes with cutting up and dividing fruit or chocolate chips . . . It's amazing to me how readily they are grasping the concept of one-fourth meaning one of four equal pieces that make up a whole. I think it's the chocolate chips; chocolate is an unmatched teaching tool!

My least favorite: Laundry. When you have two babies, then two toddlers, then two little kids who like to paint, you do A LOT of laundry. It's not exactly my favorite activity. But a couple of years ago Molly invented the sock game. It started simply and has gotten more involved as they have gotten older. It started out with matching up pairs and then counting how many pairs of socks we had and how many that made when we added one more to the pile. Now we do all kinds of fun things. How many of the socks are red? Of the total number of socks, how many are red?

Eight out of 16. Does it look like there are as many red socks as there are all the other colors? That's half. So 8 of 16 is the same thing as 1 of 2 . . . You get the picture. Once we conquer fractions, laundry is going to help us with percentages.

Math also crops up in building conversations, since Jacob loves his measuring tape and tools. And even in toothbrushing—that's actually turned into "math with a moral." They love looking at my silver fillings and talking about how many of my teeth have cavities (because "Mommy didn't brush her teeth as good as we do!") and how many don't. We have little dental mirrors, too, and they love to count my top and bottom teeth and then each other's. It's a little nerdy, but as I write this, I'm realizing just how many math conversations we have a day. Egg timer, here we come.

Why This Matters

Children need lots of experiences to make sense of numbers and counting; mathematical picture books are a terrific way to give them these experiences.

Young children are natural learners, whether it's language or math. They are "designed" to construct their own understanding about symbols, quantity, and relationships. Thanks to recent research—especially that of Elizabeth Spelke at Harvard University—we know a lot more about the innate capabilities of babies. As Spelke puts it, "There are some forms of knowledge that humans get 'for free'" (Talbot 2006). She found that just as babies are born with a structure in the mind to understand language, they come into the world with an innate ability to understand numbers. Continuing research supports her work overwhelmingly: "At first blush, it seems far-fetched that infants could recognize simple numbers and math," says Dr. Lewis Lipsitt, a developmental psychologist at Brown University. "But now, in view of a number of corroborating findings, it makes sense" (in Goleman 1992). It turns out that, among other things, babies can do a kind of addition and subtraction, track small numbers of objects, and reason about what happens when one is added or taken away (Talbot 2006).

The best way we can help babies—and toddlers and young children—build on the incredible abilities they are born with is to give them experience playing with math concepts, numbers, and symbols. Just like letter symbols, number symbols are an important part of our everyday world. Number symbols "stand for" something that isn't present; even before young children understand "how much" numbers stand for, the more experiences they have with numbers, the more natural these relationships become (Sophian 2004).

As parents and teachers, we all want to help children become familiar with what numbers are, understand their relationships, and see the ways they help us in our everyday lives. Just as you sprinkle alphabets throughout the house, including play areas, it's easy to include an assortment of objects to practice counting skills, like colorful cubes and dominoes. Children also love to measure—with clocks, calendars, or measuring cups. Play is great for forming numbers and shapes, and making patterns. Blocks are a welcome place to learn math, too—especially geometry. You can provide a variety of shapes for building, including cylinders, cones, and cubes. It's easy to make your own blocks with boxes and wallpaper; just wrap leftover boxes of all shapes and sizes in wrapping paper or wallpaper, using strong packing tape to secure the edges.

When children are engaged in play, they have many chances to learn math and practice the kinds of skills that support mathematical understanding. That makes it fun! They'll associate numbers and learning math with enjoyment and positive experiences.

A great place to start with books for kids is exploring the symbols that make up our whole world—letter symbols (in English and other languages) and number symbols are the blocks that reading, math, and all forms of communication are based on, and exposure to all of these symbols from birth makes kids more literate in each and every aspect of life.

CHAPTER 6

Relate It to ME!

One thing that never fails to make a kid LOVE a book is finding themselves in it. Their name, their favorite color (what else could possibly explain the astronomical popularity of the rather empty Pinkalicious [Kann and Kann] book series?), their hometown, a kid who has a family or a pet like theirs.

It's not so astonishing that finding a connection to the world and our place in it is a big incentive to keep reading. I still get a charge when a character in a book loves the same obscure thing as me, and I still get tears in my eyes when I read about characters who feel the way I do.

These are some of the books and ways that we have found for the kids to connect with books through shared names, loves, hobbies, passions, or situations. It has also been a wonderful way for me to introduce things to my kids that are important to me, and for me to feel that they are getting to know me better (even if they don't realize it yet—they're only six, and I'm still just Mommy, not a real person).

What's in a Name

Our names are a key piece of our identity. I feel that for myself, and I certainly see it in my children. I love this quote from Madeleine L'Engle (in *A Wrinkle in Time*, 1962, p. 47): "If your name isn't known, that's a very lonely feeling."

My children and I not only respond and feel ownership when our name is spoken to us, but feel a sense of camaraderie with someone else who shares our name, whether in life or in books. We had a book with a Molly character in it, quite by chance, and it bothered Jacob so much that there was no Jacob in it that we had to rename one of the characters Jacob. (He made me get a pen and write it in above the other name, so I wouldn't forget to read it that way.) We make a point of looking for books with characters who share their names, and they really adore those books.

Try finding books for your kids featuring characters who share their names—but don't stop there: expand to family, friends, and teachers. They'll find it hilarious, and it might introduce them to genres and topics that might not otherwise catch and hold their interest.

Here are some examples of the books *our* family loves that feature our names. Molly's favorite Molly characters are the ones in *Tough Chicks* by Cece Meng (2009), *What's the Big Idea, Molly?* (2010) by Valeri Gorbachev (and *Molly Who Flew Away*, 2009), and *My Name Is Not Isabella* (2010) by Jennifer Fosberry (because her middle name is Isabelle, and this is about the "toughest, bravest, smartest," etc., girl in the world).

Jacob has a few favorites, too. The one that gets read the most is *Jacob's Tree* (1999) by Holly Keller, since it's about a Jacob who wants to get bigger and measures himself on a special tree. We have a growth chart in their room, and every time we read the book, my Jacob runs to see if he's gotten taller yet, too. We also like *Jacob O'Reilly Wants a Pet* (2010) by Lynne Rickards and *Jacob and the Magic Feather* (2004) by Deborah Hartman, which is about not only a Jacob, but a Jacob who goes hiking in the White Mountains in New Hampshire, which is where I grew up, so both Jacob and I feel a special connection to this book.

Just in case you have a Meghan (Megan, Margaret-called-Meg, etc.) in the family, here are my own favorites: Meg Murray O'Keeffe from Madeleine L'Engle's series, Meg March Brooks from *Little Women* (Alcott 1868), and of course Meg from the Meg and Mog books (Nicoll 2012) (a delightful little witch and her cat).

How to find these books? Personal knowledge, friends, and family. Librarians are always a great resource. That's where I start if I'm stumped. And if she (or he) comes up empty, our search plan is usually to look for books about the different names at online bookstores, where books are usually ranked by popularity and a search for a name will give you authors and characters other people love, which is a pretty good place to start.

Princesses, Trucks, and Other Favorites

Maybe you have a little boy who has no interest in books, but loves to play with cars and trucks. Simple solution: get him a great book about cars and trucks! *Cars* (2009) by Robert Crowther is awesome—the pop-up cars one—because it has moving pieces and a pop-out racetrack. That's an obvious one. But there are a million ways to marry whatever hobby, idea, person, animal, or indulgence occupies your interest to an existing or burgeoning passion for the printed word.

Of course, your own children will have their own particular interests. But many kids, at one point or another, have a passion for princesses, superheroes, or both. So we have over the years developed these lists of favorites that have been big hits on the birthday party gifting circuit. If you've got a mini–caped crusader or a plucky princess at your house, one of these lists may appeal to them!

Plucky Princesses (and Other Fabulous Girls)

The Princess and the Pea by Lauren Child

Not every princess book features an actual princess, but *The Princess and the Pea* has the original independent and strong-willed princess and is a great place to start—especially this gorgeous and funny version by Lauren Child. If you're not familiar with Lauren Child's other books, especially the Charlie and Lola series, that's a whole other fun set of books to explore! Lola is a very funny and determined little girl in her own right.

Eloise by Kay Thompson, illustrated by Hilary Knight

She may not actually be royalty, but try telling Eloise that. Eloise is six. She is a city child. She lives at the Plaza. She lives a fabulous life! Eloise is the inspiration behind many of the newer precocious little girls (like Olivia, Nancy, and Lilly), and you just can't, can't, can't imagine anyone who will make you laugh, laugh, laugh harder. For more online fun with Eloise, try Eloise, the Animated Series website (www.meeloise.com/) or the Eloise Official Website (www.eloisewebsite.com/).

The Paperbag Princess by Robert N. Munsch, illustrated by Michael Martchenko

This is a wonderful book on many levels. The main character is a beautiful princess with beautiful clothes. Then something happens and all she has to wear is a paper bag, and she has to save her prince (who is less than appreciative, and frankly, less than princely). Without being the least bit preachy, this book encourages young girls and teaches all kids great lessons about being resourceful, strong, courageous, determined, and what actually constitutes a happy ending.

Lilly's Purple Plastic Purse by Kevin Henkes

Why do little (and big) girls want to be princesses? Sure, there are the pretty dresses, crowns, and castles. But the real draw is the freedom a princess seems to have to do things her own way—her own creative, wonderful, determined, sometimes weird, and always special way. Lilly is a modern princess, whose high-spiritedness sometimes gets her into trouble but whose lovable nature helps get her out of it.

Olivia by Ian Falconer

Just like the little girl in your life, Olivia is good at lots of things. One of those things is wearing people out. Another one is charming them. *Olivia* is one of the simpler books on the list, with perfect pictures for the youngest princess, and is also funny and charming enough to enchant older kids and adults. Luckily, there are several more Olivia books to delight you when everyone has memorized this one. (No, Olivia isn't technically a princess, but don't tell her that!)

Do Princesses Wear Hiking Boots? by Carmela LaVigna Coyle, illustrated by Mike Gordon and Carl Gordon

Some little girls want to be a princess, but maybe without the fancy dresses and courtly manners. (See also *Princess Pigsty* [2007] by Cornelia Funke.) Maybe your little princess likes hiking boots and scraped knees. This fun and inclusive book ends with a mirror and the (slightly sappy, but completely true) adage "A princess is a place in your heart."

Priscilla and the Pink Planet by Nathaniel Hobbie, illustrated by Jocelyn Hobbie

Although some princesses like hiking boots, others like all things PINK. And this delightful book gives you every shade of pink, with funny rhyming text and pictures that may remind you a little of Dr. Seuss. This is a really fun way to indulge a child's love of pink, while introducing them to the beauty of other colors, and simultaneously avoid those boring pink-for-the-sake-of-pink books (like *Pinkalicious* [Kann and Kann 2006] or *Double Pink* [Feffer 2013]).

Fancy Nancy by Jane O'Connor, illustrated by Robin Preiss Glasser

Nancy is one fancy little girl. The bad thing is that no one else in her family is half as fancy. The good thing is that they have Nancy to teach them. Their love for her is evident in their willingness to play along, and her love for them (even with exasperation) shines through in the end. This first entry in the Nancy series is a great one, and the sequels almost match it. The best part of the book is the whimsical, playful, and detailed illustrations. If they look familiar, it's because Glasser also illustrated *You Can't Take a Balloon into the Metropolitan Museum* (Preiss 2001). If they don't look familiar, go find that book, too! It's formidable, which, as Nancy could tell you, means "great" in French.

Mini–Caped Crusaders

Superheroes are popular characters, whether you are a grandmother remembering Mighty Mouse, or a *Sesame Street* alum with fond recollections of Super Grover. Today's littlest book lovers have a handful of great young heroes and heroines who try out their superpowers, real or imagined. Treat your young caped crusaders to the adventures of Ladybug Girl or Mighty Max. The following books are terrific inspiration for creative play.

Ladybug Girl and Bumblebee Boy by David Soman and Jacky Davis

Ladybug Girl takes on the world of the playground, where she enlists the help of Bumblebee Boy; in this familiar world, they zoom all around, looking to help anyone in trouble from Scary Monsters to Mean Robots. Known to their parents as Lulu and Sam, these two superheroes fly through the sky (as they swing higher and higher), save Lulu's dog Bingo, and even take on a Giant Snake. "Nothing can stop us!" they cry—a wonderful slogan for today's young superheroes. The artwork is really fun, and the story is charming for adults as well as kids. This sequel is even better than the original *Ladybug Girl* (which we all also love).

Mighty Max by Harriet Ziefert, illustrated by Elliot Kreloff

Max loves playing hero, worrying his parents that he might hurt himself with his daredevil adventures as Evel Knievel, Superman, and even King Kong. On a day at the beach, he decides to become his own superhero and save the day as Mighty Max. Max's adventures in his imaginary world are captured perfectly in the childlike and whimsical crayon illustrations.

Superhero ABC by Bob McLeod

What could be better than meeting 26 superheroes, from AstroMan to The Zinger!? Although this book has the bright look and feel of comic books, it has the wonderful illustrations and the playfulness with language you expect in a high-quality picture book. It has the added attraction of playing with letters and sounds, with heroes like Upsidedown Man, who wears his Uniform Under his Underwear, or Ms. Incredible, whose superpowers allow her to become Invisible in an Instant. We are particularly fond of Laughing Lass and the Volcano (who Vomits on Villains). Silly, creative, and fun for the whole family.

Timothy and the Strong Pajamas by Viviane Schwarz

Timothy really wants to be strong—and he'll do whatever it takes, like drinking milk, exercising, and thinking strong thoughts. When his mother fixes his favorite pajamas, he magically has the super strength he needs—and uses his powers for good, with the help of his trusty stuffed monkey. In the course of his adventures, he loses—and regains—his superpowers. Timothy is a wonderful superhero, dedicated to helping his friends.

Max by Bob Graham

Max comes from a whole family of superheroes. His parents, Captain Lightning and Madam Thunderbolt, provide everything he needs to fly: a cape, a mask, and lots of support and encouragement. But Max prefers to walk on the ground, thank you very much, to the bafflement of his family and the taunts of his classmates. In the course of the book, Max emerges as a "small hero doing quiet deeds." The cartoon pictures really add to the story and make it fun to share with young superheroes. It's a good read-aloud, too.

A Taste of Home

It shocks me that my kids are Californians. A big part of my identity is being a New Englander (hardworking, slower to make friends but keep them for life, totally uncomfortable talking about money, Sox and Celtics fan to the death). Somehow in my head I skirt the fact that I've now lived in Los Angeles longer than anywhere else, and that my kids were born and (so far) raised here. They don't own cold-weather clothes, have played in the snow exactly once when visiting Oregon, and even think they like the Lakers. So it's probably not as subconscious as I think that I've introduced to our home library a few children's books that remind me of home. Introducing the kids to those seemingly unimportant and funny things like accents and attitudes I grew up with has become both important to and special for me—it's showing them a side of myself, the same way we listen to show tunes in the car and spend at least an hour a day cooking together.

The Wicked Big Toddlah by Kevin Hawkes

I love reading this book, with its sprinkling of words like *wicked* and pictures of maple-tree tapping and flannel-wearing relatives. The kids love the funny touches they look for in the pictures, like how Toddie needs a garden hose and helicopter to have his diaper changed. And New Englanders and New Yorkers alike will love the sequel, *The Wicked Big Toddlah Goes to New York* (Hawkes 2011).

Duck Duck Moose by Dave Horowitz

Other Horowitz books, like *A Monkey Among Us* (2004) and *Five Little Gefiltes* (2007) were already huge hits at our house, so we took this one home from the library without even cracking the spine. I was even more delighted than the kids to find that it was about a moose who heads south with his duck friends for the winter when he realizes everyone else is departing or hibernating and even the Pancake Hut is closed. This book had me at the "I heart NH" T-shirt.

Ox-Cart Man by Donald Hall, illustrated by Barbara Cooney

I love this book. As a kid, it reminded me of the Little House series (Wilder) and of visiting Plimoth Plantation. I was thrilled to rediscover it with my own kids and find that they too love this simple story of a man and his family who toil all winter to sell things in town so they can buy items they can't make to get through another winter. (If you're new to Hall's work, try reading his collection of essays about growing up in New England, *String Too Short to Be Saved* [1999], yourself. I adore it.)

A Farmer's Alphabet by Mary Azarian

This is one of those alphabet books that belong equally on the coffee table and a child's bookshelf. It's a beautiful book, and it depicts a lovely lifestyle with simplicity and honesty. It offers tons to talk about, from making up stories about life on the farm to accompany each illustration, to discussing the woodcutting technique used in the book. Azarian also illustrated one of Donald Hall's other beautiful children's books, *The Man Who Lived Alone* (1998). That book has made me cry every single time I've read it, from the time I was five right through to just now, when I reread it to test myself.

Blueberries for Sal by Robert McCloskey

I was tempted to put my favorite McCloskey book on the list (*Make Way for Ducklings*, 1941), but I took the kids blueberry picking once when they were little, and we rediscovered this book and have really been enjoying it. Sal and a little bear cub are out with their mothers gathering blueberries for the winter when each loses their mother. Even if blueberry picking isn't a part of your childhood memories, this may leave you thinking about which summer produce says "SUMMER!" to you (blueberries and corn for New Englander me, tomatoes and watermelon for my New Jersey–raised husband) and seeing if you can take your kids to pick and eat that (or some other local summer treat) fresh. We've been enjoying doing that as a family and sharing our own memories (verbal and visceral) with our kids.

Where did you grow up? What did you do as a child? Are you a city kid or a country kid? Did you play certain sports or take part in specific activities? Think about the things in your childhood that helped inform who you are and that are different from how or where your kids are being raised, and seek out some books that will introduce your childhood to your kids.

Favorite Colors

"Grandpa, you are wearing green, green, green, just for me!" Molly beams whenever Grandpa Jim wears his green bike T-shirt. Which is often, since her doting grandpa will do anything for a chance to see that devilishly cherubic smile.

"Grandma, you can knit me any of those sweaters, as long as you knit it red, 'cause that's my favorite color," Jacob announces, faced with a choice of sweaters from a pattern book. And Grandma happily obliges.

Ever since they were tiny, Jacob and Molly have not been shy about letting the people around them know their preferences—including colors.

These are some great books to share with babies and children that celebrate color:

My Many Colored Days by Dr. Seuss, illustrated by
Steve Johnson and Lou Fancher

This simple, elegant book brings colors and images together with emotions and moods. Paintings cover whole pages in deep color with engaging couplets that children appreciate. Don't expect the cartoonlike images that illustrate Dr. Seuss's usual books. Steve Johnson and Lou Fancher create more abstract art, very fitting with the message to young children about the acceptability of their moods and emotions. "You'd be surprised how many ways/I change on different colored days," the main character tells us. Most colors are also associated with an animal. Red is a horse kicking up its heels. Brown is a bear, "slow and low." On a yellow day, "I am a busy, buzzy bee." On a green day, he's a "cool and quiet fish." On a happy pink day, he's a flamingo! And in the end, "I always go back to being me."

Mouse Paint by Ellen Stoll Walsh

When three mice discover paint, the fun begins. Their "mouse paint" find leads them to climb right in, dipping their toes in other colors and creating whole new combinations. When the red mouse does a jog in a puddle of yellow paint, his feet turn a bright, cheery orange. By the end of the story, they are mixing all kinds of paints and colors and creating lovely hues to delight in. The cut paper collages are bright and peppy, and there's lots of subtle humor (like washing themselves clean in a bowl that has "CAT" written across it).

A Day with No Crayons by Elizabeth Rusch, illustrated by
Chad Cameron

This book is an ode to color—and to imagination. When young Liza uses her lovely white walls as paper and draws all over everything enthusiastically, her mother (not surprisingly) takes away her crayons for the day. Without her beloved crayons, Liza feels her world has become gray—but bit by bit, she discovers color in the world around her and that she can create art in the way she sees. The message is that art is everywhere! The text is engaging, too, so it makes a lovely read-aloud and sparks discussion on the colors and textures in our daily lives.

Hailstones and Halibut Bones by Mary O'Neill, illustrated by John Wallner

Lyrical poetry and imaginative artwork go hand in hand in this now classic collection of 12 poems that evoke a world of color and its relationship to all our senses. The title is taken from the stem of the poem: "What is white?" My mom introduced this book to me when I was four, and I was captivated from the start. Time for the next generation of poets and artists.

* * *

Molly and Jacob would never forgive me if I didn't include their favorite color books:

Grandpa Green by Lane Smith

A picture book by one of our favorite authors, Lane Smith, is always a reason to celebrate, but this one is special for a lover of the color green like Molly and her own loving grandpa. This tale is told through the eyes of Grandpa Green's great-grandchild, who tells the story of his ancestor's whimsical topiary garden. It's fun to unpack the hidden symbols in the topiary—each spread is packed full of fun and ideas as the biography of Grandpa Green unfolds.

Red Truck by Kersten Hamilton, illustrated by Valeria Petrone

"Red Truck is a tow truck, a work truck, not a show truck . . ." Hardworking Red Truck has to save a stuck school bus full of kids. This is a great read-aloud for the truck-loving crowd, filled with rhymes and lots of sound effects! The quirky drawings are reminiscent of J.otto Seibold, but for slightly younger readers.

Why This Matters

> Sharing books that have special emotional attachment—because of place, like a New England upbringing, or interest, or the special recognition of personal names—helps build a stronger bond and pleasure in the reading experience.

"Your baby's [and child's] attention to how much pleasure you find in books is one of the greatest benefits of looking and listening to a book together" (Stamm 2008, 117).

Making connections between our own lives and the experiences in books is the heart of reading comprehension (Pearson, Roehler, Doyle, and Duffy 1992; Keene and Zimmerman 2007). Reading researchers now know that it's crucial for very young children to see themselves in books—and know that "the important stuff" in their lives will help them understand the stories in the books they share with family and friends. Children need to have their knowledge and experiences validated to associate enjoyment with the books they explore. This is an important foundation that allows them to anchor their new learning when they are exposed to new ideas and concepts. They learn that they bring themselves to the books—even when they jump into culturally or conceptually unfamiliar books and stories.

Making connections to books can also really help develop children's cognitive skills. When they hear about an event or situation through a book, conversations that follow the reading can help them describe similar situations in their own lives, building from a foundation of knowledge. They can use those connections to remember the past. For example, after reading a book about visiting the zoo, children can remember both events and feelings when they went to the zoo. They can learn to make predictions as well, based again on their own knowledge from similar situations.

Finally, making personal connections to others through books and stories helps develop important empathy skills. By age three, children picture what others see and feel. Early experiences are critical in developing empathy (Epstein 2012). Adults can help model that awareness of and sensitivity to others through making explicit connections to understanding the feelings of the characters in books. This helps children learn that others share their feelings and acknowledges their capacity for empathy.

CHAPTER 7

Have Some Fun

I am always trying to find ways for the kids and me to have more fun with books. Whether it's reading in silly voices, playing games with letters, or finding books to read that I love more than they do, it's important to find the fun and keep it silly.

Ministry of Funny Voices

If Monty Python had their funny walks, every parent has a bag of funny voices. Most are to keep kids interested and involved in the story—so I tell myself. In truth, I often find myself returning to books that keep *me* interested by letting me read aloud in fun, silly, or different voices and accents. Reading in silly voices comes naturally for my husband and me—we both have training in acting and have worked in the entertainment industry. But, just in case performing for your kids isn't your strong suit, I want to recommend some books that all but force you to dip into your bag of silly voices:

Cowboy Baby by Sue Heap

It's gettin' late and time for bed, but Cowboy Baby needs to round up his animal posse. Then he and Sheriff Pa play a game of hide-and-seek, and Sheriff Pa lassos a twinkling star for his little deputy before tucking in the tuckered-out baby. You can hear the Old West music playing in your mind as you read aloud the lyrical text. Then tuck your own cowpoke into bed.

Tough Cookie by Dave Wisniewski

This is one of those fun books that appeals to two-year-olds (who like the idea of talking cookies), to eight-year-olds (who get the parody a little better), and to parents, who channel their own versions of Bogie and Bacall in reading aloud this funny story of a cookie who lives in the jar, see? But there's this guy "fingers," see, who comes and snatches the cookies . . . Can he and his gal Pecan Sandie and the lowlife crumbs at the bottom of the jar save the latest cookie that "fingers" has set his sights on?

I Will Never Not Ever Eat a Tomato by Lauren Child

Lauren Child books are all great fun for both kids and adults. If you haven't seen the BBC show based on the books, you may not realize straightaway that Lola and Charlie live in England. But once you do, you can't help but read these with the singsong "But, Chaaaalie" that you just know the precocious Lola would use. Lola is a very picky eater who has a long list of things she will not eat, ending with the fact that she would "never not ever eat a tomato." Her savvy older brother usually finds a way to get Lola to do just what he wants (and what is really best for her).

Skippyjon Jones by Judy Schachner

Skippyjon is a cat who likes to sleep with the birds and pretend that he is a Chihuahua. When he disappears into his closet, he emerges in old Mexico to have adventures with his imaginary pals, *los Chimichangos*. Although the Mexican accents are fun, I actually have the best time reading his mother, Mama Junebug Jones (who sounds very much like Blanche DuBois from *A Streetcar Named Desire* at our house).

The Three Bears (Any version you like; we go with Byron Barton's at our house.)

This isn't only a good voice story—with Papa having a deep voice, Mama having a higher voice, and Baby having a little voice—but a great teaching tool. I heard this tip once from a child psychiatrist who was speaking at a parents' group: use this book to demonstrate a voice (or voices) that you don't like that your child uses. Papa could be really loud (a voice that should be saved for outside), Mama could be really whiny or high pitched (that voice we all hate), and Baby Bear talks just right. Then if your child uses a tone you don't like, you can say, "I can't understand you when you talk like that bear. You need to use your just-right voice like Baby Bear so I can understand you."

Any pirate book is fun, but especially *Shiver Me Letters* (Sobel 2009). No explanation necessary. Just start rolling your "Arrrrrrr"'s and have fun!

Monsters Eat Whiny Kids

One year, when the kids were about three, we were at a local children's bookstore, and Molly picked out a book the way she often does (by color—it was bright green). It was called *Monsters Eat Whiny Children*, written and illustrated by Bruce Eric Kaplan (2010). I knew I'd like it just from the title, and the illustrations are delightful (Kaplan is a cartoonist for the *New Yorker* magazine). They remind me of Quentin Blake, with a hint of Edward Gorey. The more we read it, the more I felt myself relaxing, as if exorcising some of my bad parent demons. Harping on how annoying it is to hear children whine to the very children who whine to you the most is quite cathartic. Talking about how monsters will eat them sort of lets you feel as if you are yelling at the kids and telling them they can make you crazy. But far from actually doing that (and scarring them—and yourself—for life), you are curling up with them on your lap, snuggling and laughing and enjoying a moment. You get the best of both worlds.

There are loads of books that "teach" kids lessons that I'm sure are fine, and I have used them myself in the past (books about how great it is to share, or how fun a new school is, or why hitting is never right). But they're usually pretty annoying. I much prefer books like this. *Monsters Eat Whiny Children* teaches without the preaching, and is frankly fun to indulge in. When someone starts whining, telling the offending child that a monster will eat them if they don't stop feels much better than when I yell. And if it continues, we can get the book and snuggle together and read it. Nine times out of ten, by the end of the book both of us are giggling and relaxed, and there's nary a whine or raised voice to be heard. The book will always be sitting there on the shelf for the next time the kids deserve to be eaten.

Another big problem we address with books in our house is eating. Everyone at our house loves *A Bad Case of Stripes* by David Shannon (2004), and we eat loads of lima beans whenever that book gets pulled out. Though I'm not a fan of this book, *Pinkalicious* by Victoria Kann and Elizabeth Kann (2006) definitely helps us talk about why we can't live on sugary treats alone. Offbeat books can be a great source for dealing with behavioral (or new situation) issues at home.

A Book I Don't Like

This is not a novel to be tossed aside lightly. It should be thrown with great force.

—Dorothy Parker

I don't like to be negative, in general. In particular, I don't want to be negative about books. But every once in a while there's a book that just raises your hackles. Sometimes, it's a book that gets undue worship and praise (ahem, *Twilight* [Meyer 2008]). Sometimes it's a book that you really want to like but it derails (*Her Fearful Symmetry* [Niffenegger 2010]) or never finds its footing (*A Great and Terrible Beauty* [Libba 2005]).

But sometimes it's just a book you don't like and firmly believe should be thrown with great force. And that's a difficult thing to do when it's a book your kids love. We have a book like that at our house. We got it at the used-book store just before the kids' first Easter. I thought it would be good to start building a holiday library at home, so we bought *Max's Chocolate Chicken* by Rosemary Wells (2000). *Chocolate Chicken* is an exceptionally silly book, and what makes me crazy is that the kids loved it the first time I read it to them and continue to love it to this day. I had to read that book 15 times in a row every single day, week in and week out for a solid month. I tried hiding the book and pretending I couldn't find it, but they cried till I magically managed to find it. They would forget about it, and then stumble across it. They found an identical copy at preschool and got me to read it to the whole class one day when I was subbing. We can't seem to escape that nauseating book. I keep reading it because they love it, and I want them to love books.

Why am I writing about this at all? Because to me, loving (some) books and hating (some) books are two sides of the same coin. It's about feeling passionately about the written word, and I think that's great. I encourage Molly and Jacob to find books they love, even if I don't agree. And I tell them how I feel about books, too. Once they were old enough to understand, I talked to them about how little I liked this book. I told them I will read it once in a while because I love them, but just like different people have different taste buds and like different foods, people also have different tastes in books. So I won't force Molly to listen to *Little House in the Big Woods* (Wilder 1932) (which she doesn't like, though I really, really, really want her to, since I loved it as a little girl), but she can't make me read *Max and Ruby*. Well, at least not too often—and she definitely can't make me like it.

A Comic Thing Happened

I'm not a big graphic novel or even comic book reader. Both of my brothers are, so I've tried to get into the sweeping and gorgeous graphic novels they periodically recommend, but they just don't grab me. Comic books weren't really on my radar for my kids (at least not yet, although I do have a few fond memories of reading Archie comics when I was sick as a kid, but much older than my kids are now). But I am a big proponent of anything that gets children to love and appreciate the power of the written word. So Mum and I were instantly interested when one of her friends mentioned that her son has special needs and that comic books have been a real eye-opener for her in terms of getting kids who don't have a natural affinity for reading to start enjoying books. They really help some kids visualize the story, and draw them in. And once you're in a story, who can help but love it?

Still, her recommendations remained tucked in the back of my head, unused. My kids loved books—I didn't need comics. Then my readers got a very cool present for their fifth birthday: two comic books. One was the first Tiny Titans adventure (*Welcome to the Treehouse* [Baltazar and Baltazar 2009]), and one was called *Korgi* (Slade and Slade 2007). Molly and Jacob love them. They were gifts from the five-year-old friend of theirs who is probably the best reader they know. Both kids are just starting to sound out short words and read for themselves, and one of the things they love about these books (especially *Korgi*, which has no words at all) is that the abundance of pictures and the details allow them to read the whole book to themselves. We've been tentatively exploring this world of first comics, and our whole family is finding it an eye-opening and empowering experience. (The kids feel empowered by not needing me at all to read the story, and I feel empowered to sneak off and let them read themselves to sleep while I relax with a glass of wine and a novel of my own.)

Since I hadn't even known that there was a whole genre of comics for prereaders, I'm assuming there are others in the same boat. I am by no means an expert, but here's a short list of the comic series we have discovered (so far) that are a big hit with the four- and-five-year-old crowd:

Tiny Titans by Franco Baltazar, illustrated by Art Baltazar

This is about the tiny heroes at Sidekick Elementary School. They're typical kids, just with a few extra abilities and problems.

Pooches of Power: DC Super-Pets by Sarah Stephens, illustrated by Art Baltazar

This spinoff is about the super-pets of the Tiny Titans.

Owly and *Owly & Wormy: Friends All Aflutter* by Andy Runton

These creatures have adventures of the sweet and simple variety, kind of like a comic-book *Frog and Toad* (Lobel 1984).

Johnny Boo: The Best Little Ghost in the World by James Kochalka

The best little ghost in the whole world really appeals to kids. There's burping and there are ice cream monsters—enough said.

Korgi by Christian and Ann Slade

Maybe it's that there are absolutely no words in this book. Maybe it's that the creatures in the forest are called Mollies. Maybe it's that the illustrations aren't dumbed down for kids at all, and that although the monsters make them shiver at first, the kids settle in when they realize the monsters won't ever win. For whatever reason, this is the book both kids sneak out of bed to read to themselves over and over. It's my favorite, too.

Why This Matters

> Great news! It's not only fun to be playful while reading, but actually helps babies and young children learn to attend longer, enriching the reading experience for everyone involved.

One of the things early childhood researchers have discovered is that changes in pitch, accent, or pace when reading to children add variety that encourages both the bonding and the attention.

So reading in "funny voices" isn't just goofy—it actually nurtures children's brain development (Stamm 2008; Tallal 2004).

Children appreciate—and learn from—the exaggeration at the heart of dramatic reading, whether it's silly voices or indulging your inner drama queen with squeaky, gruff, or whiny voices.

It's also important that you show genuine enjoyment yourself. Choose books that you enjoy reading and playing around with! That enthusiasm is contagious; when you're having fun, it motivates your kids to have fun with reading, too. They'll remember these early experiences and bring what you've modeled to their own independent reading. You can also encourage them to join in the fun with you right now, role-playing the funny characters—and voices.

The more interactive you are with books, the better the chances of increasing playful enjoyment. Making up new endings to familiar books can be a lot of fun for you and your young audience. You might ask your child what kind of new ending they want today—happy, funny, scary, mysterious, silly? It doesn't have to be the ending, either—you might "help the author" by changing the middle of the story, adding a new character, or changing the climate or setting.

Even if you aren't comfortable giving a performance, being enthusiastic in your reading and avoiding a monotone shows kids you are engaged, attentive, and enjoying yourself. Book-reading activities that stimulate emotional, auditory, and visual connections in the brain also stimulate the parts of the brain that process and store language. So go for it! It's fun for you—and great for your kids.

CHAPTER 8

Let's Get (Meta)Physical (Books About Books)

B ooks! There is nothing that good readers love as much as losing themselves in a great book. What about reading some books about the temples for books (those underfunded and disappearing local libraries), the guardians of books (again, the underpaid and disappearing species of librarians), the writers of books (including your kids), and even books about being inside books?

Library Love

The library is a parent's secret weapon. Although most of us would love to have huge shelves of books at home packed with millions of books, that's not economically or spatially possible. The library lets you test-drive and explore hundreds of books to find those that your child absolutely must own. There are often wonderful and free story times or children's performers. Librarians can help you find books for your child's current obsession. Almost all kids love the library—that feeling of being in control (of the books they get to bring home) and the excitement of discovery and learning. Like the kids (er, animals?) in these books:

But Excuse Me That Is My Book by Lauren Child

All children have their favorite book at the library that they think of as theirs. Every parent is familiar with the process of renewing a book until you can't anymore and the resulting hysteria when you have to return "their" book. The whole family can relate to Lola, who LOVES one particular book at the library and doesn't know what to do when it's not there. Her brother, Charlie, tries to help her find a new book, but it seems like nothing can possibly be as good as *Beetles, Bugs, and Butterflies*. Or can it? Ironically, this was one of the books we renewed until we couldn't anymore.

Library Mouse by Daniel Kirk

Sam, an adventurous little mouse, lives in a small hole in the wall in the children's section of the library. He sleeps all day but roams the library at night, reading, reading, reading—and acting out his adventures. Like many committed readers before him, Sam decides to try his hand at being a writer himself. His little self-published books become such a hit at the library that the children invite their anonymous author to come to Meet the Author Day. Sam's brilliant solution to this dilemma is a wonderful inspiration for young writers to write their own stories and add their voices and talents to their bookshelves. The illustrations show Sam to be a delightful character, with his little mouse teeth thoughtfully sharpening pencils for the children, or his dark eyes flashing as he poses in front of the little mirror. Look for the sequel, too: *Library Mouse: A Friend's Tale* (2009), where Sam has a secret collaboration with Tom, an aspiring young author.

What Happened to Marion's Book? by Brook Berg, illustrated by Nathan Alberg

Marion, a little girl hedgehog, wants to be a librarian when she grows up. She loves her library books and carries them with her everywhere—even to the breakfast table, with predictably disastrous results. She frantically tries to clean the jam from the book, but isn't successful in salvaging it. Her cleanup efforts only ruin it further. Children love this engaging picture-book story with its large, full-page illustrations. Best of all, there are two more books in this series: *What Marion Taught Willis* (2005) and *When Marion Copied* (2006).

Tomas and the Library Lady by Pat Mora, illustrated by Raul Colon

In this true story of Tomas Rivera, readers see the influence of a librarian on a little boy's life. Tomas grew up in a migrant family, loving to read but not always having access to books. One summer, a librarian takes him under her wing and introduces him to stories about dinosaurs, and horses, and sparks his interests in a world of ideas. The colors in the vivid pictures are earthy, warm, and inviting. Children are often interested to learn that Tomas Rivera grew up to be a respected educator and chancellor of the University of California at Riverside. See also the Spanish edition (1997).

Bats at the Library by Brian Lies

Someone left the window open in the library! That's all that the bat friends (yes, the same bats from *Bats at the Beach* [2006]) need to discover to make it Bat Night at the library. These book-loving bats delight in the many wonders of the public library, from playing at the computer to making duplicates of themselves on the copy machine. But of course, the best part is exploring the books, with fairy tale pop-ups, information books, and a parade of characters from "the classics" that they read to each other. See if you can spot images from *Make Way for Ducklings* (1941), replaced with tiny bats crossing the Boston street, or a Bat-Aladdin conjuring a Bat-genie from a magic lamp. Three little bats in the corner read a (sort of) familiar board book together: *Goodnight Sun!* The detailed pictures and references to a number of books invite repeated readings, and the lilting, rhyming text makes it fun for even the youngest readers.

Edward and the Pirates by David McPhail

Edward is a passionate reader who devours whatever book is in front of him, from seed catalogues to cereal boxes to the books he discovers at his favorite place, the library. He gets so involved in his books that whatever he is reading seems to become real. When he checks out a book on lost pirate treasure, the pirate characters come to life at night in his home, demanding the book from him so they can find their buried treasure. Though he won't give it to them (after all, it's checked out on his library card!), he does agree to read the story aloud to them. Very dramatic illustrations add to the adventurous spirit of the book.

Inside a Book

For my daughter, the worlds of books, or of her own creation, are often far more real to her than reality. One day we were playing one of our car games, where we take turns telling stories. Molly was telling us a story, and it suddenly took a very sad turn. The kid in the story was lost and missing her parents. And Molly started to cry as she was telling it. I said, "Honey, if this is making you cry, you can change the story. *You* are telling it—you can make it happy!"

She shook her head sadly, and through her tears said, "Mommy, I can't! I can't change the story; this is the way the story is. It is just a sad, sad story. It has to be. It won't be changed." Now, that's a storyteller! The story is already dictating itself to her. She isn't in control (and she thinks she's in control of pretty much everything). For kids with wild imaginations, the line between fiction and reality is wonderfully blurred. The notion of characters in books coming in and out of our world—or us going in and out of theirs—isn't fantastic at all; it seems natural.

In a typical work of fiction, the characters remain blissfully unaware that they *are* works of fiction, and they don't interact with either their authors or their audience. But when the fourth wall is broken, we can enter the world of the book in an entirely different way. These books allow you to lose yourself by getting *inside* them. In some instances the characters become aware of us (the reader) and pull us in by speaking directly to us. In others, the authors have chosen to treat their own fictional beings as real people who become dragged (wittingly or not) into books or book worlds.

For kids like Molly, this seems natural, and it's fun for them to see that other people view books and characters this way. For kids who appreciate things being more by the book (like Jacob, who is our rule follower and enforcer, our little logic-stician), this opens up a whole new way of interacting with books.

After reading one of these books, it's time for a fantastic metaphysical family discussion. What if we are really characters in someone's book? Would you live differently? What would you do? Is there a book world you'd like to read yourself into? Which one? Why? And finally, can you write (or draw or tell) a story about meeting some of your favorite characters?

We Are in a Book! by Mo Willems

This is one of our favorite (recent) books—all three generations in our family. It's everyone's favorite worried elephant and upbeat pig, but in this book, something is different. They notice something new: someone is watching them. Is it a monster? No, it's a READER! They play tricks on the reader and are thrilled to be read, until they realize something terrible . . . Books end! Yet in a lovely twist (that works every time, at our house) they come up with a wonderful solution.

There Are Cats in This Book by Viviane Schwarz

What a playful interactive book. Children get to open flaps and frolic with three frisky kittens: Tiny, Andre, and Moonpie. And these cats let you know how they want to play with us, the readers. On each page they instruct you in what's to come on the next page—or let you know they want to go back a page and play with that yarn again! Bold, bright colors and sturdy flaps make this a practical and inviting book that readers will want to read again and again. In fact, the cats beg you to come and play another day. We never read this book without also reading the sequel, *There Are No Cats in This Book* (2010). In this one, Andre, Tiny, and Moonpie want the reader (you!) to help them play *outside* the book. The good news is, you help them succeed, and they even send you a postcard from outside the book to share their adventures. The ongoing dialogue between the cats and the readers is even more pronounced in this follow-up.

The Monster at the End of the Book by Jon Stone, illustrated by Michael Smollin

Many children are introduced, unwittingly, to the study of metaphysics by Grover in this Golden Book classic. Grover has heard that there's a monster at the end of the book, and asks the reader not to turn any pages, getting us all closer to the monster (he is afraid of monsters, of course). He cajoles and begs, all to no avail, as children gleefully turn page after page until we get to the end of the book to find Grover—a furry, lovable, and thoroughly embarrassed little monster.

A Book by Mordecai Gerstein

A little girl and her family live in a book, but she doesn't know what kind of story she is in; there are so many already in the book. Her mom is a firefighter, her dad's a circus clown, and her brother is going to grow up to be an astronaut. Even the pets have their own story. But what is hers? When she goes off in search of her story, she brings us along; when she realizes that we are there with her, she lets out a big *Eeek!* "What is that huge . . . blobby thing that looks something like a face?" It feels a bit creepy to her. On her travels, she encounters fairy tale characters, including the Three Bears, but she's pretty sure she isn't in a fairy tale. She meets a detective, who thinks her story may have been stolen . . . (Guess who the famous literary detective is.) This is a very original book that toddlers enjoy, yet with enough humor and fun that even third or fourth graders like reading it on their own.

Why This Matters

> Any book that helps invite us as readers into the characters' lives—and even into the plot itself—helps create that almost out-of-body experience of being so engrossed in a book that you feel as if you are there.

What better reading experience can there be than being "lost in a book"? Whether it's a simple picture book that encourages readers to make wet cats fluffy by blowing on them, like *There Are Cats in This Book*, or one where the characters actually start talking to you and are unaware that they are fictional, like *A Book*, books that place the reader "inside" are terrific for nurturing the kind of special "flow" reading experience that committed readers live for. Children see their actions—and their worlds—having an impact on the books, which in turn affect them.

It's wonderful preparation for future intense experiences with reading. Book lovers have been known to talk back to characters in books, reacting to them as if they were physically present. Reading theorists claim that such readers have created a new mental "space" that Mary Jacobsen calls "literary space" (1982). Inhabiting that "literary space" is a sign of deep involvement and comprehension of the text.

PART THREE

Traditions, Rituals, and Celebrations

I f you are like me—and most of my friends—you often find yourself reminiscing about your childhood days. Grandma's fried chicken every July 4, special coffeecake every Sunday morning, weekend trips to the lake, stockings left out for Santa (or sneakers for the solstice elves, believe it or not), and bedtime stories every night. When we become parents, those memories of family traditions return to us. Rather than missing the many little traditions that embodied our childhoods, why not consciously establish some routine "customs" as a way to create new memories and bond with our families? There are many small ways to bring traditions into our daily lives—they'll be the things our children remember as they grow older and likely pass on to their children.

Another wonderful aspect of traditions is that the very nature of a tradition relies on repetition—and anyone with young kids knows that repetition is their lifeblood. Kids adore the reassurance and order of repetition. They know it has happened, is happening, and most important, that there's an implied promise from you that it will happen again—we (as parents and teachers) are always here and will continue to provide that continuity (and love and support). You can ALWAYS find a way to work a book into anything—so of course many of the traditions we follow at our house and in our family incorporate books.

CHAPTER 9

Family Traditions: The Call of Books

My brother was visiting recently. We are close, but I get to see him only about once a year. I was a little annoyed at him when we were talking, because he kept picking up a book to read during our pauses between sentences. As I was about to call him out on it, I realized that I do this to my husband (to his great annoyance) every night. My brother and I both have to read. I see Molly doing the same thing, at night in the hallway when she can't sleep. She's curled up in the faint light of the kitchen with a book. Jacob wakes up before the rest of the family, and you can often find him reading a book in the living room. When I see this, I just about burst with happiness, because I know that finding a book and using it to keep you company is a family tradition that is already instilled so deep inside them that they will carry it forever—and ideally pass it down to their kids.

Many of our family traditions are like this; they aren't linked to holidays, but they do involve books and reading. Some of these traditions have been handed to me from my grandparents and parents, some are ones I have developed in our daily life, and one is even something my kids made up, based on a favorite book.

Inscribe It

When Molly turned three, her favorite book was *Where the Wild Things Are* (Sendak 1963). Every time she got the book out and opened it up, she would say, "Bob and Ailene give this to you." My cousin Ailene and her husband had given the book to the children on a recent visit, and it made me smile every time Molly did it. About half the time it would turn into a conversation about them and how fun their visit was. She still knows exactly *who* gave her the book and *when*, since this book (and many of the other books) have been inscribed with the giver's name and the date.

One of my own favorite books is a word book that I have from my childhood. The book is a little Hallmark thing, cute, but nothing special. What makes it one of my favorite books is the inscription on the first page: "To Meghan on her first birthday, Love Grandma and Grandpa Shagoury, February 1975." I would have absolutely no memory of that book or who it was from, but those simple words infuse it with a whole lifetime full of memories and meaning.

It has become part of our reading practice to look at the first page of a book and talk about the book's origins. Sometimes the book is an old one of mine, and it leads to stories about when I got the book, if I liked it at the time, who gave it to me, and other "When Mommy was a little girl" stories. Sometimes it's a book that was a gift to the kids when they were tiny or on a recent birthday or other holiday (we have some goofy books signed by "The Easter Bunny" that I think will crack them up when they're older and can recognize my handwriting) that evokes those memories. Inscribing the books not only gives them special meaning and memories, but gets the kids thinking and telling their own life stories. Before we read the story of the book, the kids often jump in, telling about their lives—turning them into active participants and storytellers before the first word of the story is read.

Inscribing books is something we've always done in my family, from my grandparents to my parents and now with my kids, and it's something we pass along with the gifts we give, as well as the ones we receive. Often we ask someone to sign a book for the kids if they're here with us when we open the gift. If it's not a practice in your family, I'd suggest giving it a try. Inscribe your gift books to your children with a personal note, giving the date and reason for the gift (even just a simple, "This made me think of you"). If you receive a book from someone else, once the gift is opened, consider asking them to sign the book for your child. It'll give everyone one more reason to treasure and love that book.

One little tip: if you're giving the book as a gift, don't sign it till they open it! If they already have the book, they can't return a signed duplicate. If they live far away and you won't be seeing them soon to sign the book, check with the parent first, or think about getting some bookplates. You can write the note on the bookplate, and have them put it in the book once they open it.

Yes Day

I love it when we get inspired to do something from a book. That's what happened with *Yes Day*. When the kids were two, we read a book called *Yes Day* by Amy Krouse Rosenthal (2009). Yes Day is about how parents say "No" to everything all the time, and once a year the little boy gets a "Yes Day" when his parents say "Yes!" to everything. My kids thought it sounded like a great idea (surprise, surprise!). So we told the kids we would have "Yes Day" for their half birthday, which was conveniently coming up a few weeks after we first read the book. As the day got closer, we got worried. But we prepared the kids: we wouldn't say yes to anything that would hurt them (like eating only candy or not having to hold our hands to cross the street). I also started planting ideas in their heads by saying, "If you said, 'Mommy, can I have sushi for lunch?' what would I have to say?" and they would yell "YES!" and giggle. I prepped them with fun ideas that I knew they'd like and kept them thinking in tune with things I actually would say yes to. And you know what? IT WAS AWESOME! Yes, it was mainly about eating things we don't usually eat (and certainly not all in one day), but it was really nice to let them feel so in control for a day, and fun to revisit the book after we had our own Yes Day.

Yes Day has now become an annual tradition in our house. Every August we celebrate this invented holiday, and in addition to showing the kids that life can imitate art, it's taught them that we can invent our own traditions and holidays.

Jacob, our little planner, often comes up with invented holidays or games. "Mommy," he said at dinner one night, "I think there should be a holiday for celebrating fire trucks and utility trucks. And we could look for them on the street and come home and make a fire-truck cake, like we saw on YouTube. I think that would be a good holiday." You know what I said? "Yes!"

Bedtime

Most families that make time each day to read do so at bedtime, so this isn't exactly a revelatory suggestion. But what I want to suggest is that you make it more than just a nice but harried part of your bedtime routine—something that falls by the wayside if everyone is too tired or was out late at a birthday party or the babysitter puts the kids to bed. We make bedtime reading more than a routine; we made it a family tradition by incorporating these principles: make it special, make it sacred, and give it definition.

Make It Special

Too often, parents are more tired than the kids at bedtime, so parts of the routine get shoehorned or swept aside. I'm guilty of it far more than I like to admit. The kids are finally in jammies, with teeth brushed and bedtime water drunk, ready for the tuck-in. Then one pipes up: "Mommy! We forgot the bedtime story!" I groan. I admit it—I groan at the thought of *reading to my kids*. Only in my head, the phrase *reading to my kids* becomes *prolonging this bedtime routine until I'm so tired that I snap and the kids go to bed crying and I desperately need a glass of wine*. But it is a book they've asked for, and it is part of bedtime, and I can pretty much never say no to a book. So I say, "A short book." They know this means a book from the "short shelf," which is their board books that they don't want to part with, all of which I can recite from memory with zero inflection in less than a minute. Duty fulfilled, book read, now please (to quote that insightful best seller), *Go the F**k to Sleep* (Mansbach 2011).

I have read to them, but I have not made it special. And I vow anew, every time this happens, to try to start the bedtime process a few minutes earlier, put them to bed a few minutes later, pinch my arm a few times to stay awake, and read something with my full attention, in my best range of voices, and do all I can to make it special.

Make It Sacred

Then there are the times we just skip it. Sometimes for "valid" reasons (it's the Fourth of July and we're out late for fireworks and the kids fall asleep on the way home, a babysitter is putting the kids to bed, it's a birthday party, we have company, and so on). Sometimes it's just because I'm too tired or cranky. Once we even took away bedtime reading as a punishment. (I'm still mortified by that, but on the plus side, it does make me happy that the reason we resorted to that was that no other behavior modification techniques were working. In desperation we said we couldn't read at bedtime unless they behaved, and that outraged them so much that they cried, "Not that! We'll listen!" But then they didn't and we had to follow through, which I think in the end upset us more than it did them.) The reason I put valid in quotation marks above is that a *valid* reason cannot possibly exist.

Bedtime reading should be sacred. Tired and cranky? Like exercising when you're too tired, reading when you're too tired will actually energize you. Likewise, more often than not you'll find that a cranky disposition melts away with a sweet kid curled up on your lap, laughing at a favorite book. Out late? Tuck a short book (mini–Beatrix Potter books are perfect for occasions like this) into your purse and read it in the car before starting home. It relaxes everyone. Out of town or away from home? Call them and read over the phone.

Giving reading this kind of weight and importance as a family tradition that is unbreakable teaches kids the intrinsic value of reading in a way that can't be taught with words, only actions.

One evening, shortly after tucking the kids in with no bedtime story and feeling pretty terrible about it, I was catching up on a little online reading. I came across an article in the *New York Times* titled "A Father-Daughter Bond, Page by Page" (Winerip 2010). The article talks about a father and daughter reading aloud every night for more than 3,000 days—until she went away to college. I found it amazing and inspirational. If you have trouble interesting your kids in bedtime reading, or find yourself in need of a little encouragement, try talking about shooting for a "streak" with your kids. If it's a game, and you keep nightly count (perhaps even rewarding yourselves when you hit milestones), you'll all find yourselves more invested. And if you miss a day, make a funny big deal of it and start over.

Give It Definition

Growing up with a little brother meant many of our family traditions incorporated turn taking. For example, I prefer Scotch pine for Christmas trees, whereas my brother favors Douglas fir. In the way that only siblings can argue (about things only sibs argue about), we used to have knock-down, drag-out fights about which to pick, until my parents instilled the "every other year rule." And that turn taking stretched to many other things—including who picked the bedtime book. Now I see that same dynamic playing out with my kids, and we have a very strict turn-taking, book-pick rule at our house. The only difference is that I also get a turn (otherwise we'd read the same books over and over, and I can take only so much *Captain Underpants* [Pilkey 2002]). Try letting everyone in the house take turns picking a book, even a pet. Seriously—it will get kids laughing when they're arguing over books if you put them on the floor and see which the cat curls up on or the dog sniffs. We are a dander-free home and have only fish, so one night when the kids were fighting over *A Bad Case of Stripes* (Shannon 2004) and *Firefighters A to Z* (Demarest 2003), I couldn't think of how else to stop the fighting and said, "How about we let Fish Molly and Fish Jacob decide?" (Yes, our fish are named after the kids.) We held up the books and the hungry fish swam closer to one book. Both kids dissolved in giggles and agreed that the fish had picked *Stripes*, and we read that book first with no more tears.

We also try to give our book picks definition in another way: variety. In my adult book group we try for variety—a classic, a mystery, a play, a best seller, and then perhaps a biography, just to keep ourselves from falling into a rut. We aim for the same thing at home: I seek out and offer up books that vary in length, classics that I loved as a kid, new books I haven't read yet, sequels to favorites, and the occasional book of poetry (Shel Silverstein is a favorite right now); I'm hoping eventually to mix up genres. You can also ask your kids to help mix it up. Jacob is really into patterns right now. He turns everything into a pattern—Legos, what he eats, what games we play—you name it, he can turn it into a pattern.

We recently finished reading *Pippi Longstocking* (Lindgren 1945), which both kids adored. He asked if there was another Pippi book. I told him that there was, but maybe we should read something else first and then come back to Pippi. He dug his heels in, as only a five-year-old can. I sensed a serious bedtime/overtired tantrum coming. Then inspiration struck.

"Like a pattern," I said. "We can read one new book, and then a sequel to a book we have already read."

He picked up that thought and ran with it. "Yeah. We can read one Pippi book, one fireman book, one Pigeon book, and then another Pippi book. And then a fireman book . . ."

One final thought: make it lasting. Get inspired by that amazing father-daughter streak, and don't let them outgrow it. They can start reading aloud to you. You can read Shakespeare aloud as a family. You can read baseball stats in the summer. But read together as long as they live in your house. And when they move out, read when they come visit.

Cooking

I love to cook. That's a good thing, because I've been the primary caretaker of the family since the kids were born, and I'm responsible for feeding four people (all with different tastes) at least three times a day. So as a family, we've spent a lot of time together in the kitchen, literally since the day they were born. (See Photo 9-1.) To relieve my own boredom, I would drag their little

Photo 9-1: Molly and Jacob help out in the kitchen.

bouncy chairs into the kitchen whenever I had to cook anything and explain to them exactly what I was doing. It was basically my own cooking show. That's probably why at 18 months my kids developed their own kitchen game (they called it Smell Dat, and I will absolutely be pitching it to Hasbro as a game in the future), and by the time they were two, they could recite (in order) the ingredients for chocolate chip cookies. Today, their favorite thing to do is help me cook in the big kitchen and cook for themselves in their little kitchen.

There are a million reasons that cooking with kids is a wonderful thing. It teaches numbers and math, nutrition, sharing, and taking turns. It also promotes literacy; Molly is as given to curling up with a cookbook to "read recipes" as she is with one of her own books. Most of all, it is just a fun thing to do together. In our family, cooking, finding cooking books and books about food, and incorporating food into every celebration (like ALL the ones you'll read about in this chapter) has become a bit of a family tradition. For every single holiday or occasion that comes up, the kids start dragging out the cookbooks. Our tradition is finding food to go with everything we could possibly celebrate—and that food research starts in a book, cookbook or otherwise. We also use books to inspire our cooking, because it's so easy to fall into a rut with what we cook and eat. Reading *Mary Poppins* (Travers 1934)? We talk about how yummy those gingerbread cookies that Jane and Michael help Miss Corry paste into the sky and turn into real stars must be. Then perhaps the next day we'll make our own gingerbread star cookies. We love to turn books to food and food to books, no matter the inspiration or occasion. Here were some of our favorite books that propelled us straight to the kitchen, to get you started on your own cooking and reading feast. (See Photo 9-2.)

Mr. Cookie Baker by Monica Wellington

This is a fun book with great pictures and cookie recipes at the end. I can't vouch for the tastiness of the cookie recipes, since I

Photo 9-2: Eating and reading *Bee-bim Bop!* After reading *Bee-bim Bop!* we sat down for a Korean meal.

have millions of my own that I'm pretty faithful to, but I can promise that if you want to make some sugar cookies from this or any recipe, you and your kids will have a wonderful time cooking, rolling, decorating, and baking together.

Everybody Bakes Bread by Norah Dooley, illustrated by Peter J. Thornton

Carrie experiences the different breads of the families in her multiethnic neighborhood when she is sent on a rainy-day errand to borrow a "three-handled rolling pin." In pursuit of her impossible goal, she tastes seven different kinds of bread as she visits with her neighbors. Doesn't your mouth water at the thought of the coconut bread from Barbados and the corn bread from South Carolina? The pictures are cozy and inviting, and realistically show the range of ages, nationalities, foods, and lifestyles of different families. Actually trying out the recipes and baking the breads adds to the experience. If you enjoy this book, you can try Norah Dooley's other books in the series, like *Everybody Serves Soup* (2004) and *Everybody Cooks Rice* (1992).

The Red Hen by Rebecca Emberley, illustrated by Ed Emberley

Red Hen finds a recipe for "simply splendid cake" and invites her friends to help her make it. In this wonderful telling of the classic tale, Red Hen asks her friends for help at every step: gathering ingredients, baking the cake, frosting and decorating. Their response is always, "Not I" (except for the frog, who always says "Bribbit"). Of course, once it's baked, they are all willing to "help" eat it. It's a silly, fun story that will amuse and entertain—and delight everyone with the bright and humorous illustrations. And then you can bake the Simply Splendid Cake in your own kitchen.

The Blueberry Pie Elf by Jane Thayer, illustrated by Seymour Fleishman

Who isn't a sucker for wee creatures that live, unbeknownst to us, in human homes? (Think *The Borrowers* [Norton 1952)].) In this reissued 1950s book with charming illustrations, Elmer the elf lives with a family of bakers. He doesn't care for pumpkin pie, and apple pie is ho-hum, but one day there is fresh-baked blueberry pie. He jumps right in and simply swoons from the taste of those berries, eating until his little elfin belly bulges. The next day, he wants more, but the family has eaten the leftovers for breakfast. And, poor guy, no one can see, hear, or feel an elf, and he has no way to let them know his new fondness for blueberry pie. No spoilers here: will he find a way to get more of this delicious pie? The book makes you itch to bake—and eat—a blueberry pie.

Family Sing-Along

Whereas I am the cook in the family, and that's the activity I usually work into every holiday and activity, my husband is the musician and brings music into everything we do. I love music, but since a stint with flute in grade school, I don't play anything. The kids love music, too, and it's a wonderful activity to explore with books and to work into everything we do.

Music has become another tradition in our family, and we find songs that fit occasions, holidays, or interests in books or online at every opportunity. Cooking and music happen to be our family traditions—but they may not be yours. Below, I have listed some great books to get you exploring music with your family, but I also encourage you to think about your favorite activities, and ways of using books to explore those passions, share them with your kids, and make participating in, celebrating, and reading about whatever it is you love a tradition for your family.

Where Have All the Flowers Gone: A Singalong Memoir by Pete Seeger

This isn't really a children's book, but as a book for a family to share, it can't be beat for learning about Pete Seeger's life and work through his songs, journals, sources of inspiration, and references to the politics that shaped him and his art. Sit down with your favorite young ones and pore over the pages of this book while listening to the songs. You'll all be inspired by this brave singer and social activist.

When Bob Met Woody: The Story of the Young Bob Dylan by Gary Golio, illustrated by Marc Burckhardt

This biographical picture book focuses on Dylan's youth in Minnesota, in the days when he was still Bob Zimmerman. As a kid, he loved music but had no use for lessons, teaching himself to play both piano and guitar. When he was 19, he was so drawn to Woody Guthrie's music that he hitchhiked across the country to visit him in the hospital. Guthrie became his mentor, in both life and music. The illustrations by Marc Burckhardt are a wonderful and joyous look at the young Dylan as he grows from a small-town kid to an aspiring performer to a genuine folksinger in the center of it all in Greenwich Village.

Pete the Cat: Rocking in My School Shoes by Eric Litwin, illustrated by James Dean

Pete the Cat (from *Pete the Cat: I Love My White Shoes*, 2010) is back, and this time he's rockin' in his school shoes as he heads to school. Each new page has some clues about where Pete is headed next in his school day and lets kids guess where that might be, and then Pete sings about what he's doing there—always in his school shoes. The pictures are bright and fun, and the song is catchy and irresistible. Not feeling musical enough to come up with your own tune? Listen to author Eric Litwin sing the song with a bunch of kids at www.youtube.com/watch?v=nUubMSfIs-U.

Jazz on a Saturday Night by Leo and Dianne Dillon

The Dillons have created a rhythmical, lyrical, magical tribute to jazz. All the greats are here: John Coltrane and Charlie Parker on sax, Thelonious Monk on piano, vocals by Ella Fitzgerald, trumpet by Miles Davis, drums by Max Roach, Stanley Clarke on bass. The bright colors in the illustrations and the musical patterns to the language make the music come alive—even before you pop in the accompanying CD. The CD highlights jazz instruments one by one, giving a short description followed by the sound each instrument makes, then concludes with a jazz song with lyrics that match words from the book. On top of all this, it is a delightful read that kids simply love.

Mysterious Thelonious by Chris Raschka

This is a book to sing, swing, and sway to. It's an original tribute to Thelonious Monk, with beautiful watercolors that match the chromatic scale dancing over the pages. The way the words are scattered over the page make it impossible not to read it rhythmically. Readers will want to know—and hear—more about Monk after this exciting introduction. As the hand-lettered text says, "He played not one wrong note, not one . . . He played the music of freedom. Jazz is the music of freedom."

The Peter Yarrow Songbooks by Peter Yarrow

The songs in these four books were selected and arranged by Peter Yarrow (of Peter, Paul and Mary). Each book in the collection has a different theme (Folk Songs, Sleepytime Songs, Let's Sing Together, and Songs for Little Folks). They are accompanied by a CD of Yarrow singing the songs, lyrics, guitar chords, fun illustrations, and historical notes. Our kids pore over the books, picking what we'll do first, their dad pulls out his guitar, and we have a family sing-along. Even if no one in your family plays music, I'd highly recommend getting these books. First of all, you can easily use them to sing along with the CD. If you aren't ready for that step, you still will appreciate having the words to those classic songs we all somehow absorbed in our childhoods but whose lyrics we can't always remember. I can't tell you how many times I've been tucking the kids into bed when they're tired (or sick) and I'm exhausted, they've begged for "one more song," and my mind has gone blank. I usually try to remember the songs that are in these books, and then I'm good to go for another round (or seven) of "one more song." One final note about these books, or any books that have music written out or show chords or charts: that's another fascinating form of literacy for kids. Show them the language of music and how to read it and write it; when we did this at our house for the first time when the kids were still fairly young (maybe three), they spent days afterward "writing" their own music notes on charts and singing it back to me. It was amazing for me, and pretty empowering for them, since writing a series of circles and lines was much easier than trying to write words. They thought their writing looked more like the originals than when they tried to write the alphabet, and felt quite accomplished.

Why This Matters

Kids love traditions and family rituals, because they foster a sense of belonging and security. Children also thrive on routine, and rituals support that need.

All parents know the importance of predictable routines in their child's everyday life. The meals, bedtimes, activities, and naps of course depend on each child and each family, but a schedule of events helps provide a needed framework for the day.

Linda Gillespie and Sandra Peterson (2012) wrote in a recent article that the time, predictability, and emotional tone of rituals give the child, parent, and caregiver a sense of comfort and control: "They help the child manage or regulate the unsettling feelings evoked by change and draw the child and the parent closer with each reassuring repetition" (p. 77). The role of adults in a young child's life is reinforced, creating and deepening the bonds.

Why are traditions and the rituals that create them so powerful? One big reason is that they provide regularity and a sense of order, which in turn makes kids feel safe. When kids feel secure, their anxiety goes down and they can focus instead on learning and growing. When children know what to expect and have the feeling "this is the way my family does things," it helps them make sense of the world and create a predictable and soothing system. One of the wonderful—and necessary—aspects of family traditions is that they are culturally appropriate because families create them by sharing information about their ways of handling routines.

Traditions serve as markers. When families make a habit of spending a certain amount of time together, the memories seem to become automatically linked to those traditions or customs. In addition to fostering feelings of intimacy, traditions make it easier for family members to recall shared experiences.

Incorporating books and literacy into our family traditions helps link positive emotional memories with reading. Books can also act as conversation starters and spark discussions; connecting these discussions with family traditions creates deeper experiences and memories.

CHAPTER 10

Special Celebration Days, with Books in Hand

In fact, there are even holidays celebrating books! Although we use most holidays as an excuse to discover more books (and books as a way to learn about holidays), there are actually several holidays dedicated solely to reading and books. How fabulous is that? There are probably even more than this, but these are the four we celebrate every year at our house.

Read Across America

A small reading task force at the National Education Association (NEA) came up with a big idea: if we have celebrations for all kinds of events and holidays, and hold rallies for sports at schools, why can't we have a rally or holiday that celebrates and gets kids excited about books and reading? They decided to hold this event on Dr. Seuss's birthday (March 2), and the very first Read Across America was held in 1998. Now the NEA, Random House, the White House, and the Department of Education work together to promote and celebrate Read Across America.

The purpose is to get each and every family to read aloud to their children on this day (and every day). If you already read aloud every day, you can pick some specific way for your family to celebrate. In our family, we read a Dr. Seuss book we haven't read before. My kids are still quite young, so that's not a difficult task. But the man was a frightfully prolific writer, and once you start looking, you'll probably find several hidden treasures that you missed along the way. A few have been discovered and published in the last decade—most recently *The Bippolo Seed and Other Lost Stories* (Seuss 2011)—so that's a good place to start. Whether your child is 16 months or 16 years old, you will be amazed at how much they enjoy a family Seussical read-aloud.

Three other suggestions for celebrating:

- Buy a new book. Something to commemorate a day in celebration of reading. Something hardbound. Something classic or by a favorite author. Something you can keep on the shelf and inscribe. In this day of e-books and borrowing, a beautiful, classic edition will give a child a great start to building a library they will have forever.
- Find a read-aloud for the whole family, something that everyone can enjoy together. This sounds like a tough task—some families range in age from newborns to grandparents. But actually, it's amazing how many books we can all enjoy, albeit at different levels and in different ways. Here are three of our family's favorite read-alouds, all quite different, that I think will give you a good idea of the variety of books that can be shared and appreciated by the whole family:

    Fartiste, by Kathleen Krull and Paul Brewer (2008), had all three generations in our family doubled over laughing, from Grandpa, who had tears rolling down his face, to Molly, who pranced about pretending to be a "fartiste" herself. This true story of

Pujol, a performer from France at the end of the 19th century, documents his rise to fame as he learned to control his intestines to the point where he became a sensation at the famed Moulin Rouge for his "symphonic farting." It's funny, interesting, and on a topic that holds the attention of 2- to 102-year-olds—everyone in the family will gather around for this book.

Alice's Adventures in Wonderland by Lewis Carroll (1865) is probably the most obvious book that appeals to all ages in a family. It's the classic book that intrigues on many levels, with silly storytelling that is not silly in the least and is based on many true situations, stories, and people. There's sense behind the non-sense, and if you read it as a bedtime story, young kids will go to bed giggling, and older kids (or just the adults) can stay up and scour the Internet or an annotated edition to discover and discuss the method that lies behind the madness. And speaking of the Bard:

A Midsummer Night's Dream by William Shakespeare is a book, as I've mentioned before, that I have read to the kids, on and off, since they were first born. I love the language, and I discovered that the kids do, too. Although they may not sit still for 45 minutes of it at a go (the way they will for *Captain Underpants* [Pilkey 2002]), they will happily listen to a speech or two at a time, and I like to think it's seeping into their brains and lodging there, quietly percolating until it either makes sense or just gets quoted at an opportune moment.

- Read a book "pairing." We often read "book pairings" at our house. I find a book for the kids and then one for myself on the same topic, to educate myself further so I can answer their increasingly sophisticated questions on the subject. I started doing this when I first read the kids *Little House in the Big Woods* (Wilder 1932). I was wondering what else happened in Laura's life once the books ended. So I read *Laura: The Life of Laura Ingalls Wilder* by Donald Zochert (1977). It turns out her life was endlessly more fascinating than her books. Ensuing controversy notwithstanding, so many people told me to read *Three Cups of Tea* by Greg Mortensen (2007) that I finally did, and loved it. When *Listen to the Wind* (Mortensen 2009) came out, I got it for the kids, and we read two versions of the same story. Now I'm also looking forward to reading—and one day sharing with the kids—*Three Cups of Deceit* (2011), Jon Krakauer's look at the truth of Mortensen's story. When Molly and Jacob fell in love with *The Ballad of the Pirate Queens* by Jane Yolen (1998) and began asking me questions that five-year-olds ask—"But why did she . . . ? But why, Mommy?"—I went out and got *Pirate Spirit: The Adventures of Anne Bonney* by Jeffery Williams (2007) and *The Only Life That Mattered: The Short and Merry Lives of Anne Bonny, Mary Read, and Calico Jack Rackam* by James L. Nelson (2004). I'm not sure I gave much better answers (you try explaining the motives of "lusty pirate wenches" to preschoolers), but I definitely enjoyed myself, and could talk about the lives and behaviors of pirates in a more informed manner.

International Children's Book Day

Following up the US-centric Read Across America a month later comes International Children's Book Day (ICBD), established on Hans Christian Andersen's birthday (April 2) in 1967. The holiday was created by the International Board on Books (IBBY), in Switzerland, to inspire a love of reading and to call attention to children's books. Each year a different National Section of IBBY has the opportunity to be the international sponsor of ICBD. It decides upon a theme and invites a prominent author from the host country to write a message to the children of the world, and a well-known illustrator to design a poster. For example, in 2012, Mexico was the sponsor, and the 2012 theme (by author Francisco Hinojosa) was "Once upon a time, there was a story that the whole world told."

There are many possibilities for celebrating this holiday. Here's an example of one way we have celebrated in the past:

When the kids were very young, we focused on the fact that it was Hans Christian Andersen's birthday. I'm a big fan of several of his stories, but *The Princess and the Pea* (Child 2006) and *The Emperor's New Clothes* (Andersen and Burton 2004) have always been my two favorites. Lauren Child (she of Charlie and Lola and Clarice Bean fame) has a fabulous and beautiful take on the *Princess* that I highly recommend, and it's hard to go wrong with almost any version of the *Emperor*. Last year we graduated to trying to incorporate the "International" part of the holiday into the celebrating, and we read *The Ugly Duckling* retelling by Rachel Isadora (2009a). The story takes place in Africa, and the details illuminating African clothing, people, animals, and landscapes are fresh—and bring some nice diversity to the bookshelf. Isadora has a whole collection of retellings, including *Hansel and Gretel* (2009b), *Rapunzel* (2008), *The Princess and the Pea* (2007) and others. If you're tired of showing your kids only the white Disney-fied princesses and heroes, these books are a great discovery.

National Fairy Tale Day

Ever heard of National Fairy Tale Day? Well, I hadn't either, until I had kids. It's probably a completely made-up holiday—I saw it publicized a few years ago by a couple of local bookstores who were holding events for kids, and it struck the new mom in me as a fabulous holiday to celebrate. Celebrating National Fairy Tale

Day on February 26 has become a Rose family tradition, and I think that it's a holiday your family should adopt as well.

What's not to love about a fairy tale? Kids love the predictability of the beautiful heroine and handsome hero who meet some kind of evil, triumph, and live happily ever after. It's often the first kind of story kids tell, as a jumbled mishmash of plots that invariably end with the chorus of "and they lived happily ever after . . ." One day we happened to be in a bookstore with a friend and her daughter, who is roughly the same age as Molly and Jacob and was going through the Disney princess phase in a pretty hard-core way. Those horrid Disney books of the movies are magnets for kids, and after reading two aloud to them, I begged off, and my friend dutifully took her turn. I tuned out as she was reading, but snapped back to attention as she reached the end and I heard her say, "And Flynn and Rapunzel got married and lived happily ever after and went to college." She caught my raised eyebrow and grinned. A friend of hers with older daughters had told her that the only way she could choke out the books her girls begged for was if she added ". . . and went to college," because she hated it ending with marriage as the happily ever after. It may be silly, but my friend said she couldn't resist doing it as well, and I picked it up from her. It may not stem the princess tide, but it sure feels good.

Want some ideas of ways to celebrate this holiday? Here are two ways we have celebrated in the past:

- Tell a fairy tale in a round. This is the easiest way to get kids telling their own story, since it has such a comfortable and familiar format. "Once upon a time there was a very funny princess with big green eyes who loved Groucho Marx," the story might begin for Molly. I toss it from there to her, and she giggles, recognizing herself, and continues. She might want to add only a sentence, or she might continue the story for 10 minutes, rambling along. Either is fine with me, unless Jacob clamors for a turn. A couple of fun things to notice when telling stories in the round is how much they pull from familiar tales yet make them their own. Or they have no compunction about cobbling together elements from several of their favorite stories. It's also interesting how much they put of themselves into a story. Stuck? The kids aren't the only ones who can borrow from the greats—you can always move along a dragging plotline with an enchanted animal, wicked witch, or meddling fairy . . . and if tears or a fight erupts, any story can be quickly resolved with "And then it was all better, and they all lived happily ever after."

- Read a few versions of a favorite fairy tale, and see how different authors or different cultures interpret a story. Then let the kids tell or write *their* version of the tale. Cinderella is perhaps the most popular and retold fairy tale of all time, and here are some of our family's favorite versions of the story:

Cindy Ellen: A Wild Western Cinderella by Susan Lowell, illustrated by Jane Manning

Although the story is familiar, the setting is completely different in this Western version of Cinderella. The cowboy dialect is particularly fun, as we meet Cindy Ellen's father's ornery new wife and her mean new stepsisters. Cindy's fairy godmother helps her find her courage at the local rodeo. Cindy Ellen is a durn good cowgirl, and you'll take a likin' to her, once she follows her fairy godmother's advice and "quits her tomfool blubbering" and gets her "rip-snortin', gravel in the gizzard gumption."

Prince Cinders by Babbette Cole

There are other Cinderella stories that do a gender switcheroo (another good one is *Bubba, the Cowboy Prince* [Ketteman 1997]), but this is probably the funniest of them, and the one my kids enjoy the most. Poor Prince Cinders is scrawny and relatively hairless, unlike his big, hairy and supposedly handsome older stepbrothers. His drudgery is cleaning up after them while they carouse at the Palace Disco. Unfortunately, the fairy who shows up to help him isn't at the top of her game, and his sports car is toy sized, his suit is a swimsuit, and making him big and hairy turns him into an ape. In the course of it all turning out right, he meets a princess and loses his trousers, and his stepbrothers are turned into house fairies.

Cinder Edna by Ellen Jackson, illustrated by Kevin O'Malley
Cinder Edna lives next door to Cinderella. And although they share misfortunes, they don't share attitudes. While Cinderella spends all her free time weeping at her misfortunes, Edna works even harder and earns some spare change. She doesn't need a godmother—she has her own determination, and she puts a pretty dress on layaway. No glass slippers for her, but she doesn't mind. Her penny loafers are more comfortable and practical. Edna meets the prince's younger, more earnest, and dorky brother, and they fall in love and live perhaps more happily ever after than Cinderella. They get to live in their environmentally sound cottage with their rescued kittens, eating tuna noodle casserole and having fun, while Cinderella lives in the castle, attending ceremonies and speeches, and listening to her handsome and boring husband drone on about troop formation.

Jouanah: A Hmong Cinderella by Jewell Reinhart Coburn
This Southeast Asian version takes place in a Hmong village. To help her peasant family prosper, Jouanah's mother allows herself to be transformed into a cow. When her father takes a new wife, the stepmother is so mean that she tricks the father into sacrificing the cow, and he soon dies of grief himself. Although she is treated cruelly, Jouanah's kindness is rewarded by the spirit of her mother, who is the "fairy godmother" in this tale. Rather than a court with princes and princesses, the power of this story comes from village life, including community festivals and the

farming families supporting each other. The characters are illustrated with realistic paintings that are both expressive and captivating to young children and adults alike.

Mufaro's Beautiful Daughters by John Steptoe

John Steptoe's retelling of an African folktale has many familiar Cinderella elements. The king invites the young women of his kingdom to his palace so he can choose a worthy wife. Mufaro is well known for having two beautiful daughters, who go to meet the ruler. Though both daughters are beautiful, Manyara is quite mean, whereas Nyasha, the Cinderella character, is good-hearted, kind, and generous. The king chooses the one who has a good soul, not someone whose beauty is only skin-deep. The illustrations are simply magical, showing the flowers and fauna of Zimbabwe, which can spark an interest in further investigating African cultures and countries.

Baba Yaga and Vasilisa the Brave by Marianna Mayer, illustrated by Kinuko Y. Craft

Russian children grow up hearing stories about Baba Yaga, the frightening witch who lives in a house that seems to be on stilts, although they are really chicken legs that can walk and move her home. In this Cinderella-like folktale, Vasilisa is the mistreated stepdaughter who is aided by the magical doll her mother made for her before she died. With the help of this doll, she is able to perform the impossible tasks that Baba Yaga requires of her—and of course, ultimately marries the tsar. The illustrations are reminiscent of the black-lacquered wood of Russian folk art paintings and definitely add to the appeal of the book, another wonderful read-aloud. Take time to really absorb the pictures as you read the story.

Cendrillon: A Caribbean Cinderella by Robert D. San Souci, illustrated by Brian Pinkney

This West Indian version of Cinderella is told from the fairy godmother's perspective. Here, a poor washerwoman is left a magic wand by her mother and is able to use it to help her dearly loved goddaughter. The lush tropical setting is captured in Brian Pinkney's beautiful palette of seaside colors. I really loved reading aloud this book with its lyrical language and celebration of French Creole words and phrases. The helpful index at the back explains the Creole words for interested readers.

Smoky Mountain Rose: An Appalachian Cinderella by Alan Schroeder, illustrated by Brad Sneed

Set in the Appalachian Mountains around the turn of the 20th century, this retelling features a kind-hearted and articulate hog "that knew some magic," rather than a fairy godmother, and instead of a fancy dress ball, Rose and Seb get together at a square dance. Rose's stepsisters are so mean, "they'd steal flies from a blind spider." Like *Cendrillon*, a lot of the fun is in the delightful dialect.

Yeh-Shen: A Cinderella Story from China by Ai-Ling Louie, illustrated by Ed Young

The Chinese version has most of the classic elements of the folktale: a poor, mistreated, hardworking young girl, a wicked stepmother and stepsister, a ruler looking for a wife, magical help, and a lost shoe. The supernatural help for Yeh-Shen comes in the form of a magical fish. She earns his help through her acts of kindness. Ed Young is a terrific illustrator, and this book is one of his best, with dreamy, misty, evocative paintings.

The Persian Cinderella by Shirley Climo, illustrated by Robert Florczak

Another magical combination of words and pictures. Robert Florczak's paintings are so realistic, it's easy to mistake them for photographs, and he uses traditional motifs for border designs that really enhance the mood of the story. In this version of Cinderella, Settareh is the young heroine who needs new cloth to make a dress to wear to the prince's celebrations. Instead, she buys an old cracked jug, and in a scene reminiscent of Aladdin's lamp, discovers it is inhabited by a *pari* who can grant all her wishes. Of course, she enlists his help to attend the festival in beautiful clothes and an exquisite diamond ankle bracelet, which—alas—she leaves behind. Because of her stepsisters' treachery, the jug is destroyed, and Settareh herself is changed into a turtledove. Love prevails, and her prince is able to return her to her true self. Shirley Climo, in her afterword, explains that the story comes from *The Arabian Nights* and uses authentic Persian elements: the setting—the No Ruz, or New Day, celebration of both ancient Persia and today's Iran—Settareh is a popular name for this Persian Cinderella even today, and the prince's name, which means "one who shows compassion."

Banned Books Week

For those of us who love books, nothing is more infuriating (and utterly perplexing) than the notion that any book could ever be banned. The American Library Association has created an annual Banned Books Week during the last week in September to celebrate the freedom to read and the importance of the First Amendment. One of the goals of the week is to draw attention to the harms of censorship by spotlighting the actual or attempted banning of books across the United States. This is an important topic to think about, even if it doesn't seem to be an issue in your school or community. Kids (or even parents) may not realize how many books are challenged yet not banned each year, thanks to the hard work of librarians, teachers, parents, and kids. Take this opportunity to think about books, freedom, censorship, and more—and then discuss it with your kids, no matter how young they are.

This is a list of the top 25 challenged books in the new millennium.

1. Harry Potter (series) by J. K. Rowling
2. Alice (series) by Phyllis Reynolds Naylor
3. *The Chocolate War* by Robert Cormier

4. *And Tango Makes Three* by Justin Richardson and Peter Parnell
5. *Of Mice and Men* by John Steinbeck
6. *I Know Why the Caged Bird Sings* by Maya Angelou
7. Scary Stories (series) by Alvin Schwartz
8. His Dark Materials (series) by Philip Pullman
9. ttyl; ttfn; l8r g8r (series) by Lauren Myracle
10. *The Perks of Being a Wallflower* by Stephen Chbosky
11. *Fallen Angels* by Walter Dean Myers
12. *It's Perfectly Normal* by Robie Harris
13. Captain Underpants (series) by Dav Pilkey
14. *The Adventures of Huckleberry Finn* by Mark Twain
15. *The Bluest Eye* by Toni Morrison
16. *Forever* by Judy Blume
17. *The Color Purple* by Alice Walker
18. *Go Ask Alice* by Anonymous
19. *Catcher in the Rye* by J. D. Salinger
20. *King and King* by Linda de Haan and Stern Nijland
21. *To Kill a Mockingbird* by Harper Lee
22. Gossip Girl (series), by Cecily von Ziegesar
23. *The Giver* by Lois Lowry
24. *In the Night Kitchen* by Maurice Sendak
25. *Killing Mr. Griffen* by Lois Duncan

How to celebrate: read one of these books. There's something on the list for every age—you can even read No. 4 or No. 24 to a baby. If your child is old enough, try talking with them about the fact that some people thought that they shouldn't read this book. Ask them why they think some people might think that. It's fascinating to hear what they come up with.

National Train Day

Did you know that the second Saturday in May is National Train Day? (It's also Fire Service Day in Los Angeles, and since trains run a close second to fire trucks in Jacob's heart, it's a busy day in the Rose household.) If you have toddlers, preschoolers, or early grade schoolers, this is a really fun holiday to celebrate. At major train stations in many cities across the country, there are exhibits of model trains and equipment, and loads of other activities.

Before having kids, I had no idea that there were holidays like National Train Day. I also didn't realize how fascinating trains are. The reason Train Day is in early May is that it was on May 10, 1869, in Promontory Summit, Utah, that the "golden spike" was driven into the final tie that joined 1,776 miles of the Central Pacific and Union Pacific railways. This cut the travel time from coast to coast from more than six months to about a week.

I learned that at our local Train Day celebration. Here are five fabulous books about trains that are 100 percent kid approved:

The Polar Express by Chris Van Allsburg

It's a modern classic, and there's a reason for that. Yes, it's really a Christmas book, so you may wonder why I'd say to read it in May, but it's definitely a book that brings the sense of wonder and magic of a train ride to life. The illustrations are mesmerizing.

The Little Train by Lois Lenski

Pre-twins, I knew Lois Lenski as the author of *Strawberry Girl* (2005) and the illustrator of the Betsy-Tacy series. Now that the kids adore the many incarnations of Mr. Small, I think of her as his creator. Although the books are a little dull for grown-ups, kids seem to love the details of "a day in the life," and there is something gentle and reassuring about this look at the world as it was.

The Little Engine That Could by Watty Piper

This is one of those classics that is so well known, it needs no description. What you may have forgotten is that the illustrations are charming and really appeal to kids as they look for favorite toys and ask why the different engines were mean. For days after reading it, you'll be chanting to yourself, "I think I can, I think I can, I think I can . . ." Which isn't a bad thing, really.

The Goodnight Train by June Sobel, illustrated by Laura Huliska-Beith

It's a simple bedtime story, and the repetitive and fun sounds make it a hit with toddlers. It's great for train lovers and bedtime avoiders (and most of the toddlers I know are both, so it's a double win!). "Grab your teddy . . . your bed is ready." The pictures entertain with lively animals manning the train, and the rhyming story lulls them to sleep.

And the Train Goes . . . by William Bee

This is one of those great books that appeals to parents and kids alike, provides all kinds of entertainment, and will grow with your child. We took it out of the library so many times, I finally bought it, and I'm glad I did. The first time we took it out was well before the kids turned two. That was years ago, and we still read this book often. It's got cool retro illustrations and British speech ("Please, sir, please, ma'am"), fun sounds that seem to dare you to read them with increasing speed as the book proceeds, and hidden things to find in the pictures. It's oddly reminiscent of Monty Python's cartoons, but in a kid-friendly way. If this is your first encounter with William Bee, don't let it be your last. *Beware of the Frog* (2009) and *Whatever* (2005), which is basically Maurice Sendak's *Pierre* (1991) with new illustrations, are also favorites in our house.

Thomas' ABC Book by Rev. W. Awdry

I'm not a fan of these Thomas books, but I am a firm believer that if it's a book, and kids love it, it's a great thing. And kids seem to love Thomas and this book. My kids love pretending to be the trains. And it's got the alphabet, so it gives you nice talking points for letters as well as trains.

These are three of my all-time favorites, all of which feature a train as the vehicle that kicks off the adventure.

Harry Potter series by J. K. Rowling

Would Harry have even gotten to Hogwarts without the Hogwarts Express? Harry's first trip to Platform 9¾ is where his adventure really begins, and it's the Hogwarts Express that takes him and us from the Muggle world to the magical one. I am literally counting the days until I can begin to read this series aloud to the kids.

The Railway Children by Edith Nesbit

"They were not railway children to begin with . . . ," begins the books, and reading how they came to be will have you crying at times, but laughing plenty, too. I'm a sucker for books written at the turn of the century, but even if you're not, I think you'll find that this sweet-but-not-sappy story pulls you and your whole family in. It is slightly too advanced for preschool-age kids (unless you want to explain espionage and false imprisonment to young children), but by first grade, kids are very into it, and it's amazing how timeless the old-fashioned story is. It's a wonderful read-aloud.

Knight's Castle by Edgar Eager

This was the first Edgar Eager book I read as a kid, and once I finished it, I devoured the rest. They all have a new and different kind of magic, and the sneaky magic always manages to teach a pretty great lesson mixed in with the adventure. Since Molly and Jacob are Camelot enthusiasts, a book about knights' adventures with a little magic and kids thrown in is a sure hit. I also love the fact that it introduces the characters from *Ivanhoe* (Scott 1820) and sets the stage for that family read-aloud in about five years. In this story, four children find a magic that allows their toy knights to come to life at night and for them to have adventures with them. Having just seen the movie *Ivanhoe*, they have called their toys Ivanhoe, Rebecca, Lady Rowena, Bois de Gilbert, and de Bracy, and it is these characters they adventure with. It's a great read-aloud for kids as young as 5, and fun to read again even through age 10 or 12 after reading Sir Walter Scott's classic. (And the story begins with the children taking a train ride to the place where they find their magic . . .)

Lima Bean Appreciation Day

I happen to love lima beans, and have since I was a little girl. I can eat them by the bowlful, quite happily. My mom loves lima beans and my grandma loves lima beans, so I kind of figured my daughter might like them, too. We tried them one day after I compared them to edamame (which she loves), and she tentatively liked them. I pulled out a copy of a book my mom gave me right after I graduated from college. After I read it to her, Molly realized that she wanted to be like Camilla Cream, and she too would LOVE lima beans. Now, because the boys in our family don't share our lima love, we don't eat them as often as we girls would like. When I read about Lima Bean Appreciation Day (April 20), I knew it was a great excuse to celebrate by eating one of our favorite foods and reading one of my favorite books:

A Bad Case of Stripes by David Shannon
Camilla Cream loves lima beans! But she never eats them, because nobody else seems to like them and she doesn't want to be different. She worries way too much about what other people think of her—so much that she comes down with a bad case of stripes. Because she tries to please everyone, she turns into whatever they are suggesting, from breaking out in stripes to growing tree limbs, tails, and even feathers. Finally, a wise and kind old woman—and a big plate of lima beans—help Camilla find her true colors.

    I know not everyone likes lima beans. But this is a fun excuse to use a "holiday" to try a new green vegetable and read a fabulous new book. If that's not your green veggie of choice, how about celebrating March 26, which is National Spinach Day, by eating some lovely leafy greens and reading vintage Popeye cartoon strips? Can't get the green veggies into your kids? February 3 is National Carrots Day and is a great day to read *The Carrot Seed* (1960) by Ruth Krauss, watch Bugs Bunny cartoons, and eat a meal of carrot soup, carrot salad, and carrot cake! The point is to celebrate food and eliminate one of those classic parent/child power struggles with some fun food and wonderful books. Pick a vegetable and Google it—chances are good someone has declared a day in its honor. And if they haven't, you get to create a new holiday. Then hit your local library or bookstore (or favorite search engine), and find a book to pair with it.

Penguin Day

This is a holiday I stumbled across while looking up things to do that were fun for the kids after a whirlwind of celebrating (and book reading) for Easter and April Fools Day. Their spring break from preschool happened to fall at the end of April, and I was looking for a reason to celebrate something or have a kind of mini–home school party at our house that week. Personally, I always find it easier to motivate myself and get into planning mode when I have a starting point. I took to the computer and looked for things to celebrate. It turns out April 25 is World Penguin Day (celebrated then because it's the time of year when penguins begin their annual northward migration). I could work with penguins. Molly and Jacob love the Tacky the Penguin books. I love *Mr. Popper's Penguins* (1992), and we'd never read it. And I had a darling penguin cupcake recipe I was dying to try. Sold! We found our favorite penguin books from home, hit the library to gather more, made cupcakes, read about penguins all that week, and even watched *Happy Feet* before bed one night.

These were our favorites of the penguin books we read:

Mr. Popper's Penguins by Richard and Florence Atwater

Before this was a disastrous movie with Jim Carey, it was a delightful book for kids and adults alike to read and giggle over. Mr. Popper always wished he'd gotten to travel—especially to the Poles. So he is thrilled when Admiral Drake sends him a gift: a penguin (named Captain Cook). But when one lonely penguin needs another, suddenly the two become a dozen and the Poppers are kept quite busy. It's a lovely read-aloud for the whole family.

Tacky in Trouble by Helen Lester

Tacky is not equally beloved by kids and adults, but the amount that your little one will chortle over Tacky and his many exploits makes up for his slightly high annoying factor. Tacky is not a normal penguin. He's not quiet, and he's not well behaved. But he does always manage to save the day just by being himself, which is actually a pretty good message. You may wish to remind yourself of that when you read this book aloud for the 27th time in a week.

365 Penguins by Jean-Luc Fromental

Rather like Mr. Popper's penguins, the penguins in this book multiply. They increase by one a day for a whole year, and the story manages to teach math, ecology, art, and rhymes all in one charming, oversized package. This lively and funny French import brings its own unique feel in both art and writing. How does the family deal with the penguin onslaught? Over the year, as penguins run amok in the house, the father decides to organize them—in boxes, by dozens, and even in cubic formation. The art is stunning, with comical birds shown in large, bright illustrations. And don't forget about Little Chilly—kids can search for him and his vibrant blue feet on each page.

Penguin Pete by Marcus Pfister

This is a lovely first book of penguins from the author and illustrator of the Rainbow Fish books. The story is light, and it's really the charming pictures of fluffy Pete that draw kids to the book over and over again. It's great for the littlest readers just discovering penguins, and also fun to take to the zoo; you can point out to toddlers how the birds they see in the book are real and right in front of them!

And Tango Makes Three by Justin Richardson and Peter Parnell

I discovered this book when writing about banned books. Shockingly, this story of two parents who love their baby is one of the most challenged books in the last 10 years. Seriously? People are that threatened by the true story of two male penguins who hatched an egg and have been raising a baby girl penguin together in a loving family? It's a lovely story, and important to let kids know that families can look like anything at all, as long as there is plenty of love.

Day of the Cowboy and Cowgirl

There are some obsessions that we seem to have only in childhood. Dinosaurs, knights, princesses, trucks, cowboys—these all seem to be things that we could not be more passionate about as kids, then all but forget about as adults. I guess this is partly because there aren't that many job listings for paleontologists or cowboys. But as kids, the fantasies abound.

Alongside the books and the Legos, the most used items in Molly and Jacob's room are in their costume box. Because dressing up as something often leads to questions about "How did they really . . . ?" it usually means we visit the library shortly thereafter, so I can answer their questions. One of our favorite museums in Los Angeles is the Autry National Center, and in July they have a huge celebration for the Day of the Cowboy and Cowgirl . . . I'm assuming you have a clear idea of the sequence of events that followed at our house when we learned about this: dress up as cowboys and cowgirls, visit the museum, a barrage of questions about what it was like in the Wild West, and then finding books about cowboys, cowgirls, and other assorted Stetson-wearing creatures. You can do the same, celebrating the Day of the Cowboy and Cowgirl on July 28 (or any day!). These are our favorite books:

Giddy Up, Cowgirl by Jarrett J. Krosoczka

Krosoczka is a huge favorite in our house, and this simple book is no exception. Cowgirl is a big help to her momma, in her own way, which any parent of a preschooler knows isn't always the most helpful. But Momma reassures her that she always tries, and that's what counts. Kids love the spilled eggs, the crash of the car, the fun language, and the bright pictures.

Little Britches and the Rattlers by Eric A. Kimmel, illustrated by Vincent Nguyen

Little Britches is headed to the rodeo in fine new duds. Too bad those rattlers won't let her pass without surrendering her clothing, one article at a time. Will she ever get them back, or will she have to ride in the rodeo in her underclothes? I bet you can guess. One of the things kids seem to like best is the repetition of Little Britches's name and the fun way both she and the sssssilly rattlersssss talk. What I appreciate as an adult is the no-nonsense, no-whining, straightforward way Little Britches handles setbacks and conflict.

Gingerbread Cowboy by Janet Squires, illustrated by Holly Berry

Gingerbread Cowboy is made by the rancher's wife, who is a little tired of biscuits every day. But he up and runs away from the rancher, his wife, and all the folks on the range, including the javelinas and long-horned cattle, chanting, "Giddyup, giddyup, as fast as you can . . ." until the wily coyote catches up with him. It's a fun twist on a familiar tale. We rediscovered this book after putting it away for a few years, and have loved it even more this time around. What changed? In the interim, the kids have discovered the old Bugs Bunny and Wile E. Coyote cartoons, and the idea that there are real "wily coyotes" cracks them up.

Pecos Bill by Brian Gleeson, told by Robin Williams, original music by Ry Cooder

This is actually a story told on CD or audiotape, but it's a family favorite of such long standing that I had to include it. Robin Williams tells the story of Pecos Bill, the original cowboy, in his inimitable style, and the music is perfect. (This is from the Rabbit Ears Treasury that my parents discovered 30 years ago and played for me and my brother as kids. It's a fantastic audiobook series, and makes a great car-trip alternative to a DVD.)

Bubba, the Cowboy Prince by Helen Ketteman, illustrated by James Warhola

Like *Gingerbread Cowboy*, this is a retelling of a familiar tale—this time a gender reversal of Cinderella. Bubba may smell like the cows he ropes and horses he rides, but it turns out that's all in his favor, as the lovely Miz Lurleen is looking for a real cowboy, not a pretender. Although Cinderella tellings are not in short supply, ones where it's a Cinder-fella are not as numerous. It's nice for kids of both sexes to see that it's not always the poor girl who is rescued from poverty and drudgery by the handsome prince. Sometimes the boys want to dance at the ball, and the girls (or women) get to make the choices and sweep the guys off their feet!

Armadillo Rodeo by Jan Brett

Most parents are familiar with at least one of Brett's lushly illustrated books—*The Mitten* (2009), *On Noah's Ark* (2003a), *Town Mouse, Country Mouse* (2003b)—and if you haven't read *Armadillo Rodeo*, it should be next on your list. The sweetly simple story uses armadillos' nearsightedness to launch the story of Bo, who follows a new pair of red boots (worn by Harmony Jean) to a rodeo for the first time, thinking he's made another armadillo friend. Bo's adventures are fun and funny, and the reassuring way Ma and his brothers trail after him to bring him home safely is illustrated in minute and impeccable detail in the side pictures and background.

Cowboys and Cowgirls: Yippee-Yay! by Gail Gibbons

This book is geared toward slightly older kids but really appeals to the younger ones as well. It is more factual than story based, which I thought would bore preschoolers and toddlers when I first found it, figuring it was more for me. This was not the case at all! Kids of all ages love to supply their own narratives and really enjoy learning facts that they can apply to other favorite books and characters . . . like why cowboys wear what they wear, who some famous cowboys and girls were, and much more. It was a nice reminder to me to never underestimate what kids can read and comprehend.

International Talk Like a Pirate Day

There's something special about pirates. Many young children love to focus their pretend play around the adventures and excitement of sailing the high seas and following the clues on maps to find treasure. They love to dress up with great pirate gear like hats, pirate belts, vests, and colorful bandanas. There are lots of excellent books for little mateys to enjoy, perhaps in celebration of International Talk Like a Pirate Day. This holiday parody was invented in 1995 by John Baur (Ol' Chumbucket) and Mark Summers (Cap'n Slappy), of Portland, Oregon, who proclaimed September 19 each year as the day when everyone in the world should talk like a pirate. For example, an observer of this holiday would greet friends not with "Hello," but with "Ahoy, me hearty!" Try it—your kids will love it. And here's a list for bedtime reading on International Talk Like a Pirate Day:

Night Pirates by Peter Harris, illustrated by Deborah Allwright

Go along on a nighttime adventure, with a moonlit ocean voyage where "rough, tough little girl pirates" allow young Tom to join their crew. This is a wonderful simple, rhythmic story, where the pirate children trick the grown-up pirates out of their treasure. The illustrations are captivating (no pun intended), and the lettering rolls across the pages in the same motion as the ship across the ocean waves. It's also nice for parents of little girls (and boys) to have their kids see pirate girls that "let" the boy join the crew.

Shiver Me Letters: A Pirate ABC by June Sobel, illustrated by Henry Cole

Pirates are plundering the alphabet letters, and they want more than just "RRRRRRR." This clever alphabet book is peopled with animal pirates who are on the lookout for each letter, often "hidden" near objects that begin with the letter's sound (like *gold* or *parrot*, although X marks the spot on the treasure, of course). Children love the characters, especially the pirate captain, a swashbuckling crocodile, complete with a hook!

How I Became a Pirate by Melinda Long, illustrated by David Shannon

When young Jeremy's extraordinary digging talents are discovered one day at the beach, he agrees to join Captain Braidbeard and his crew in digging for pirate treasure. They promise to have him home in time for soccer practice, so he sails forth on the high seas with this rather uncouth group of buccaneers. At first, he loves their lack of table manners, not having a bedtime, and his exciting adventures. But he misses being tucked in and the comforts of home, and persuades the crew to take him to his own backyard to bury their treasure. David Shannon's goofy illustrations are perfect with this humorous pirate tale. If you like this, don't miss *Pirates Don't Change Diapers* (2007), where Jeremy is reunited with his pirate friends for another (stinky) adventure.

Do Pirates Take Baths? by Kathy Tucker, illustrated by Nadine Bernard Westcott

Young children who are interested in pirates will enjoy this simple text, written in verse form, that answers 13 questions about the pirate life. The illustrations are cheerful watercolors and show the pirates living their energetic, adventurous—and in this case, good-natured—lives. They tie up their rivals or capture their competitors' ships only for sport. And yes, "when they smell very bad," they do jump into the sea for a quick scrub.

Don't Mention Pirates by Sarah McConnell

Another pirate girl with an adventurous spirit! Scarlet lives in the house she inherited from her famous grandma: Long Joan Silver. In this fun—and funny—swashbuckling story, Scarlet makes her brother walk the plank (into his wading pool!), sails the high seas in search of buried gold, and reclaims her pirate birthright. The energy in the illustrations adds to the playfulness of the story.

Bubble Bath Pirates by Jarrett J. Krosoczka

This book came to our attention when we became obsessed with one of the author's other great works: *Punk Farm* (2010). Krosoczka is a wonderful author who writes with a voice similar to Mo Willems and Jon Scieszka—it's that modern voice that kids love and relate to instantly. This simple book about two little boy pirates who have fun in the tub, then plunder the kitchen for ice cream, is appealing to young kids who love pirates, bathtime, and ice cream, but maybe aren't as big fans of hair rinsing or pulling the plug from the drain.

Pirate Girl by Cornelia Funke

Because Molly is our own little pirate girl (she spent several months at age two refusing to leave the house without her pirate captain hat—see Photo 10-1), I have to end with this book. It's about a feisty little girl named Molly who is off to visit her

Photo 10-1: Molly is ready for adventure in her pirate hat.

grandma when she is kidnapped by the ferocious pirate Captain Firebeard. He thinks that he and the crew of the *Horrible Haddock* rule the high seas, but there is one pirate more fearsome than he is. Molly knows who it is . . . and it's someone who will rescue her and exact a pretty terrifying revenge on the pirates who dared mess with Molly.

Why This Matters

Family rituals are part of a generational process that creates a sense of identity for individual members and reflects the family's shared belief system.

Special occasions give kids a sense of belonging, making them feel secure in their membership in the family. Barbara Fiese (2006) reminds parents that the support and sense of identity that family-created "special occasions" engender are actually "like a buoy for emotional health" (p. 97). Having these traditions over time also helps memory formation; research is showing us that talking about the past with family members, especially when part of dinners, rituals, and family gatherings, make kids' memories stronger over time (Fiese 2002).

Including books and literacy as central to many of those celebrations is a natural if you are establishing a culture of reading in your home. What a terrific time to use the positive emotions around reading books as a way to deepen relationships with family and create positive memories—and events to look forward to.

CHAPTER 11

Holidays and Books Go Hand in Hand

One day when the kids were recovering from a cold, we were curled up on the couch, snuggling and reading. Since it was the third day in a row they'd been home from preschool with runny noses and fevers, we'd been doing a lot of reading. I pried myself off the couch and headed to their room for another stack. I didn't bother to look at the books, just grabbed a pile and went back to the couch. Settling myself between them, I picked the first book from the stack, opened it, and was about to read when, "Mommmmmmeeeeeeeeee!!!!" "No, no, no, no, no!!!!!" Both kids started wailing. I was bewildered.

"What's wrong with you both?" I asked. "I thought you wanted another story!"

"Not that one!" Jacob cried.

"You are the wrongest mommy!" Molly yelled, slamming the book shut. "That is only for Christmas!"

They were right. It was *How the Grinch Stole Christmas!* (Seuss 1957), and we traditionally read that book only between Thanksgiving and Christmas. At first I wondered if they were just being cranky, but the more I thought about it, the more I realized that reading this book at a nontraditional time for them would be as strange as going on an Easter egg hunt near Halloween. This book was very closely associated with celebrating Christmas. Book = celebration? I love it. "You're right," I said, putting the book aside. "What was I thinking?"

Christmas

For me, the best thing about Christmas is all the family traditions. Some are passed from generation to generation, and some are ones that you create with and for your own little family. It's such a wonderful sense of belonging and connectedness and an amazing way to feel the ties that wind through our families across time and age. For kids, who thrive on routine and repetition, it gives them a feeling that all must be well if it's the time to do that special thing again.

In our family, books are a large part of the Christmas tradition. Although a couple of our family traditions are probably ones that every family shares, a few of them may be new to you.

Chances are good that if you celebrate Christmas, and you have one book that makes you think of Christmas or that you read annually, it's *'Twas the Night Before Christmas* (Moore 1837). In our family we read a special edition, illustrated by Matt Tavares (2002) (special to us, because it was a gift to the kids on their first Christmas from Grandma). The kids wear their special new Christmas Eve jammies (this is the one present that we open on Christmas Eve, and it's always the same thing, and it makes going to bed a little more fun), and we munch on the extra cookies from the plate we've just set out for Santa. This is exactly what we did when I was a kid, and I love doing the same thing each year and anticipate doing it every year, building on the ritual.

Here's another obvious one: *How the Grinch Stole Christmas!* (1957). We read this book often, starting after Thanksgiving, but one night during the week before Christmas, we read it and then watch the animated short movie. When the kids were two, we made it through about 10 minutes of the movie. The following year we did 15 minutes. Finally, at age four, we were ready for the whole thing, and now that's our tradition. The book can be read often and any time, but the book/movie combo is once a year, in the week before Christmas.

This one might be new to you. My favorite author is Madeleine L'Engle, and she wrote a small Austin family book called *The Twenty-Four Days Before Christmas* (2010). It's about the year that the youngest Austin child was born and Vicky's fear that Mother might miss Christmas because she is having a new baby. We read a chapter a night (the short chapters are just right for a nightly ritual). A wonderful side benefit is that as Vicky tells about each of the 24 special things *their* family does leading up to Christmas, it gives us new ideas for traditions we could do. Each year we manage to incorporate something new—by the time Molly and Jacob head off to college, we'll have co-opted all the Austin traditions.

These are some of the other Christmas-themed books that are our family favorites and may one day be yours:

A Child's Christmas in Wales by Dylan Thomas, woodcut illustrations by Ellen Raskin

The sweet nostalgia of Christmas is perfectly captured in Dylan Thomas's poignant memoir of his childhood memories. It's a perfect read-aloud for all ages because of the lyrical words and rhythm of the story. Although your kids probably won't sit still for the whole story, you can read them parts of it and savor the rest yourself. We have a feeling the twins will listen in a little longer every year. There are many different illustrated versions, but we like the simplicity of Ellen Raskin's woodcuts (plus, this little paperback was part of our own New Hampshire memories of Christmas).

The Polar Express by Chris Van Allsburg

Ride along on an old-fashioned steam train that magically takes children to the North Pole on Christmas Eve. The simple, clear-cut story is told by a grown-up looking back on his adventure, meeting Santa to see him off on his sleigh ride. The illustrations draw readers in—full page and with fantastic and magical lighting to enhance the effect. There is also a sweet central message of the power of believing: "Though I've grown old, the bell still rings for me as it does for all who truly believe." There's no better way to celebrate the spirit of Christmas than with a reading of this picture book.

Little Women by Louisa May Alcott

Little Women is considered to be the first children's novel to become a classic. Why not introduce this wonderful story to your children with an excerpt about the March family's celebration of Christmas? The first two chapters make a wonderful read-aloud. Chapter 1 begins, "'Christmas won't be Christmas without any presents,' grumbled Jo, lying on the rug." But of course, though they are poor, the four girls are able to celebrate family and fun together. Don't have the book? Check out "The Little Women's Christmas" online at www.netplaces.com/family-christmas/the-stories-of-christmas/the-little-womens-christmas-louisa-may-alcott.htm.

Auntie Claus by Elise Primavera

Auntie Claus is "so curioso." Sophie's glamorous and sophisticated aunt lives in a penthouse in Manhattan, in New York. But every year, she disappears for an extended "business trip" from right after Halloween through New Year's . . . Hmm. Auntie Claus's repeated message is about the importance of giving rather than receiving. Sophie, a bit spoiled, can't seem to hear this message until she stows away in her aunt's luggage for the adventure—and lesson—of a lifetime. Great fun.

Olive, the Other Reindeer by Vivian Walsh, illustrated by J.otto Siebold

Actually, this modern "retelling" of Rudolph is about an adorable little dog named Olive. This cute little so-called reindeer (based on the author's Jack Russell terrier) hears the "Rudolph the Red-Nosed Reindeer" song and decides that, rather than a dog, she is really "the other reindeer" and belongs at the North Pole helping Santa. Of course, Olive saves the day. It's a funny and sweet little story, with fantastic illustrations. Our favorite: Olive dangling from a ribbon on Comet's neck as Santa's sleigh flies through the sky.

Father's Day

I don't know if men get the same feeling when they watch their wives reading to their kids, but from talking to the women I know, I can tell you that one of the most swoon-inducing things that makes you fall in love with the father of your children all over again is seeing your kids curled up on their daddy's lap, listening to him read them a story. (See Photo 11-1.) I also remember my daddy and my grandpas reading to me, and how it

Photo 11-1: Molly and Jacob listen to Daddy read them a story.

made me feel like the queen of the world. It's one of those gifts that's really more for the giver than the recipient, but I traditionally give my husband a book for Father's Day. I make sure it's about a subject he loves and is appropriate for the age the kids are so he can read it aloud and share one of his interests with them. I know he enjoys it, but honestly, it's more for me and the kids. That yearly gift from me is one I think they will all enjoy.

Try giving the fathers in your life a book for Father's Day that they can read aloud to their children or grandchildren and reflects one of their interests. You may also want to try interviewing them about which books are their favorites for reading to and with their kids. It's insightful, interesting, and, if you record the interview, a lovely thing to be able to keep and give to your kids one day when they have children of their own.

Nontraditional Passover

When I was little, Christmas and Easter were holidays we loved and celebrated, but we didn't realize they were any different from Halloween, the Fourth of July, or the Red Sox making the playoffs. We were pretty much Christian in that we celebrated traditional Christian holidays, but we were not religious. Happily for me (because I love holidays) I married a man who is also not religious but celebrates the traditions of the Jewish faith. (He's also pretty thrilled with the fact that the Red Sox became more of a dynasty than a joke!) I pretty much get something major to celebrate every other week.

Both their dad and I want our kids to understand and respect the traditions of our cultures (our kids are certainly the melting pot come to life—Irish, Syrian, Welsh, and English on my side, and Hungarian and Russian from their dad), so we've tried to make all holidays a time for family and traditions. Although this always includes books, it's never more so than when it's a tradition I am still learning about—like the Jewish holidays I didn't grow up celebrating.

Since the kids were born, I've been slowly accumulating books for our holiday library that have taught both me and the kids (and refreshed their dad) about the historical meaning of Passover and how to hold a Seder dinner, as well as some fun and silly books that help bring it to life for the kids.

Whether this is a holiday that your family traditionally celebrates or it's new to you and you'd like to introduce your kids to another culture's traditions, these books appeal to the whole family.

Uncle Eli's Passover Haggadah by Eliezer Segal, illustrated by Bonnie Gordon-Lucas

This was the first Passover book we got, and we actually got it before we had kids, to acquaint me with the holiday. It is a (modified for kids and families) Haggadah, written as a rhyme in a way that reminds me of *'Twas the Night Before Christmas*. (Most of the reviews of the book compare it to Seuss, and there are plenty of nonsensical Seussical terms, but to me they feel a little forced, and I think it suffers more than it benefits from that comparison.) If you're looking for a Hagaddah to do with school-age kids (and up!), I don't think you could do better—and the pictures are a treat. In our house the kids are still a little young and we read a few pages here and there as a fun book, rather than using it at the Seder. (Our modified Seder dinner takes more like 10 minutes, and then has about 15 minutes of songs sung to tunes the kids recognize.)

Passover: Celebrating Now, Remembering Then by Harriet Ziefert, illustrated by Karla Gudeon

This is my favorite Passover book. It's beautifully illustrated and shows both the origin of the Passover tradition and how it might typically be celebrated today. Seeing the pictures linking the two really made the holiday come to life for me as someone who was not raised thinking and talking about it. My favorite example is the picture of the workers forced to build the pyramids, and then the typical ingredients that go into the charoset, which symbolizes the mortar they used.

Five Little Gefiltes by Dave Horowitz

I love Dave Horowitz (*Humpty Dumpty Climbs Again* [2011a] and *Twenty-six Princesses* [2011b]), so I was excited to discover this book. It's the tale of five little gefilte fish who leave the jar to explore New York. Just like the "Five Little Ducks" in the song, one fewer comes back each day (to which Mama Gefilte says, "Oy vey!"). Since my husband likes gefilte fish and they are at our Seder table, I thought it was a great way to introduce the kids to the concept. It's also a funny way to teach kids all sorts of Yiddish vocabulary.

The Little Red Hen and the Passover Matzah by Leslie Kimmelman, illustrated by Paul Meisel

This is a Jewish retelling of a classic story, like *Five Little Gefiltes* (Horowitz 2007), but this one is even more relevant to Passover, since the Little Red Hen decides to make some Passover matzah and begins with growing the wheat and so on. In addition to the funny Yiddish language touches (the Red Hen kvetches instead of cheerfully going it alone: "I should live so long, to see this bunch of lazy no-goodniks put in an honest day's work"), there's an updated ending that I love where everyone discovers the true meaning of Passover and redeems themselves. And there's a recipe for matzah—I'm a sucker for anything with a recipe.

Hanukkah Firsts

For the past few years, the kids and I have been discovering Hanukkah together, and we have a list of our favorite "firsts" in coming to understand the meaning and history of this holiday. Now that the kids are getting a little older, we can move on and read some more detailed histories or more complicated parables, but if your family is a young one just starting to celebrate and looking to add to your holiday library shelf, or if you are interested in celebrating another culture's holidays for the first time, these are all good introductions and wonderful "firsts."

A Very First Hanukkah Book

Dreidel, Dreidel, Dreidel Board Book illustrated by Stephen Carpenter

I hesitate to recommend this, as it's definitely one of the more annoying books we've ever owned. But the kids LOVED it. They picked it out for their very first Hanukkah, when they were about 10 months old, because when you press the button on the cover, it tinnily plays "I Have a Little Dreidel" over and over and over. But as a very first introduction to the holiday, it's kind of perfect. They learn the dreidel song, and see basic elements of the celebration (family, menorahs, dreidels, and so on) in the bright illustrations. If only it came with ear plugs.

First "About" Hanukkah Book

Sammy Spider's First Hanukkah by Silvia Rouss, illustrated by Katherine Janus Kahn

Sammy Spider and his mother live on the ceiling of the Shapiros' house, and Sammy is fascinated by watching them prepare for Hanukkah. He wants to celebrate, too! Between listening in on the family and talking with his mother, Sammy learns a lot, but he doesn't get to spin a dreidel, because spiders spin webs, not dreidels. But on the last night of Hanukkah, Sammy gets a surprise. The pictures are reminiscent of Eric Carle, which is appealing (in our family) to kids and parents alike, and the story does give kids an excellent overview of a Hanukkah celebration.

First "Heart" of Hanukkah Book

The Borrowed Hanukkah Latkes by Linda Glasser, illustrated by Nancy Cote

This is my favorite Hanukkah book, because the girl is determined and adorable, and it's really about the true meaning (for our secular family) of not only Hanukkah, but Christmas as well: it's about sharing, giving, family, neighbors, and celebrating each year by enjoying each other—and eating yummy food. We started reading it when the kids were four and beginning to understand the idea of sharing what we have with others and really acting selflessly. This book struck a chord with the kids, and whenever I read it to them, I choke up.

First Multicultural Hanukkah Book

Hanukkah Moon by Deborah de Costa

I tend to think of these holidays in the cultural terms that my husband has taught me—the Russian and Hungarian cultures and traditions that his parents and grandparents handed down to him. Until I read this book, I hadn't thought about how Hanukkah is celebrated in other cultures, so reading about the Mexican celebration of Januca, complete with the dreidel piñata (which captivated my piñata-loving kids) fascinated me, and opened my eyes.

First Hanukkah Poetry Book

Hanukkah Haiku by Harriet Zeifert

I love this book. Not only does it have the most beautiful illustrations, but it showcases something unique to do for each day of Hanukkah, it teaches kids about haiku, and it is short. You can read it together several times each night, which gives plenty of time to look at the pictures, talk about what we will do to celebrate each night, and even discuss poetry, the haiku format, and syllables.

Thanksgiving

Thanksgiving is one of our family's favorite holidays. We love the chance to get together, talk, catch up, and take part in a ritual of gratitude. Unfortunately, in most picture books (and in lots of history books), Thanksgiving is presented as an uncomplicated celebration where Pilgrims and Indians shared the bounty of the harvest. But for neither the Wampanoags nor the early settlers was it so simple. I grew up in New England, where I spent more than one holiday at Plimoth Plantation, interacting with the reenactors, who did not wear all black and buckle hats. It was with a little chagrin that I started picking up books for kids and realizing how many of them reduced this holiday to this: "Pilgrims wear black. Are good. Are hungry. Indians wear almost nothing. Live in teepees. Are good. Have lots of food. Share food with Pilgrims. Everyone lives happily together. The end."

It was important to me to find some books for kids and families that open up multiple views and bring to light more historical information. After searching through many books, my mom and I came up with this list of books that include two nonfiction historical picture books, two books with authentic Native American stories, and two books that show "a day in the life" for both Pilgrim and Wampanoag kids, to try to give myself and my family a more complete and accurate idea of what was happening around the time of our nation's "first Thanksgiving."

Nonfiction Historical Picture Books

1621: A New Look at Thanksgiving by Catherine O'Neill Grace

National Geographic created this realistically illustrated book to put aside the Thanksgiving myths and take a new look at our American history. In cooperation with Plimoth Plantation, the writers and photographers take a journey back through time to view that gathering in 1621 to celebrate the first harvest. This true history includes the voices of all the participants, including the lost voices of the Wampanoag Indians. The authors believe they have significant new perspectives to share: "There was neither cranberry sauce nor pumpkin pie at the 1621 harvest celebration. There were no Indians with woven blankets over their shoulders and large feathered headdresses cascading down their backs. There were no Pilgrims in somber black clothes and tall hats with silver buckles, either. The English didn't even call themselves Pilgrims at the time." (p.6)

Thanksgiving: The True Story by Penny Coleman

This book sets out to discover the truth behind the legends and the myths, and it was a great one for brushing up on some facts to have at my fingertips to combat the stereotypes the kids were getting bombarded with. The author examines the birth of the holiday and its path to national recognition. She also looks at the history of football games (they started on Thanksgiving in the late 1800s!), long-lost traditions, and the different kinds of meals prepared each year. It's a wonderful reminder of how exciting historical research can be, digging into primary documents and discovering surprising facts and stories. This is a good book to own, as you can read it yourself, and as the kids get older, you can read aloud different tidbits.

Native American Stories

The Children of the Morning Light: Wampanoag Tales as Told by Manitonquat, illustrated by Mary F. Arquette

A respected elder and contemporary spiritual leader of the Wampanoag tribe, Manitonquat, retells these stories from his tribe and his tradition. Each story has a full-color, full-page illustration by Arquette, a Mohawk artist. The tales tell of Creation, of a time when humans and animals spoke the same language, and speaks to the mysteries of Death, the reasons for the four seasons, migration, and other aspects of the human experience. There is both humor and wisdom in these stories, and they make wonderful read-alouds. It's not just for Thanksgiving time; this gem of a book is a wonderful addition to anyone's collection.

Giving Thanks: A Native American Good Morning Message by Chief Jake Swamp, illustrated by Erwin Printup, Jr.

The Six Nations (Iroquois) have a beautiful ceremonial tradition that is a salute to Mother Earth and all her beauty. This message of gratitude is adapted for children by Chief Jake Swamp. In simple and eloquent language, and with vivid striking images, the book shares a good-morning message that gives thanks to water, grass, fruits, animals, the wind, rain, moon, sun, and stars. The gifts of the earth stand out in the rich landscapes that illustrate the book. This is another perfect book for both Thanksgiving celebrations and for all year-round to honor the wonders of the natural world.

A Day in the Life

Tapenum's Day: A Wampanoag Indian Boy in Pilgrim Times by Kate Waters

Plimoth Plantation is a historical site that re-creates the town and daily lives of the Pilgrims in 1627. Also on the property is a historical re-creation of a Wampanoag settlement, which served as the location for the photographs in this book that illustrate "a day in the life" of a young boy living in that place and time. Tapenum is a boy young enough to not yet be a warrior, yet old enough to be disappointed by this fact. It shows how he passes his day, how members of his family interact, and how he lives. The book tends to hit you over the head with more information than story, but the details and the images really bring a different time and culture to life, and it holds a special fascination for many kids, especially around this time of year.

Sarah Morton's Day: A Day in the Life of a Pilgrim Girl by Kate Waters

A companion piece to the Tapenum book, this one chronicles "a day in the life" of a young Pilgrim girl. It's based on historical accounts of an actual girl, and like *Tapenum's Day*, the photographs for this one were taken at Plimoth Plantation. For kids who don't live close enough to visit the living museum themselves (and also for all American Girl fans), this is an excellent representation of how different life was—and how much life was "all work and very, very little play"—for children almost 400 years ago. Girls are especially fascinated by the spread that shows Sarah getting dressed in her one set of everyday clothes.

Halloween

We love Halloween at our house. We have the biggest costume box of any family I know, so the dress-up part isn't relegated to just this one day. But what is unique to Halloween is coming up with one special costume that's not just your everyday firefighter (unless you are Jacob, who has been a firefighter for three years straight and has no intention of changing that pattern anytime soon) or princess. And my typical source of inspiration is (obviously) books. Some of my favorite costumes as a kid were Mary Poppins, Maid Marian, Raggedy Ann, and Pippi Longstocking.

Aside from dressing up, the other best part of Halloween is the spooky, haunted, ghosts and goblins and witches aspect. In other words, Halloween can be scary. For some grown-ups (and older kids) that's half the fun. But for any child (or parent) who has been kept awake all night, for nights on end, by something that was scary enough to induce nightmares, the spookily stuff (as Molly and Jacob called it when they were toddlers) is to be avoided. These books are ones I sought out to introduce the spookily bits in a way that's fun for the younger set, with no worries or bad dreams in sight.

Zen Ghosts by John Muth

It's Halloween, and Stillwater the panda arrives at the home of his friends Addy, Michael, and Karl. The children are excited about the magical evening, their costumes, and their bags full of treats. Taking up a Chinese calligraphy pen, Stillwater draws a story of wonder for the children. But is it Stillwater telling the story or a special visitor? And who are the real characters in the tale? It's a not-too-scary ghost story that is based on a Zen koan that leaves you with more questions than it answers. As usual, John Muth's illustrations are gorgeous, and the writing is lyrical. Stillwater, the Zen panda who spouts haikus and gentle wisdom, is also featured in two of John Muth's other books: *Zen Shorts* (2005) and *Zen Ties* (2008).

Skeleton Hiccups by Margery Cuyler, illustrated by S. D. Schindler

What does a skeleton do when it gets the hiccups? He can't drink water, eat sugar, or hold his breath (though kids and adults will giggle to see him try). Even his friend Ghost can't scare his hiccups away. What will work? Even more fun than finding out is enjoying the silly, detailed pictures along the way. This is a great book for de-spooking the idea of skeletons.

Ghosts in the House! by Kazuno Kahora

This deceptively simple book stays with you. Whether it is the beautiful illustrations, the vibrant Halloween colors, or the charm of the story, everyone in the family will appreciate this book. Not scary at all, it's the gentle tale of a nice witch who moves into a haunted house and has a very practical application for all the ghostly inhabitants. (When winter comes, don't miss Kahora's other book, *Here Comes Jack Frost* [2009].)

Bone Soup by Cambria Evans

Witches and zombies and mummies, oh my! This delightful story features all the usual Halloween creatures, but they are rendered so charmingly, and the story is so tantalizing, that there isn't a scare in the whole tale. It's a Halloween-themed telling of Stone Soup, and a fun idea for a Halloween dinner would be to make a soup and throw in a bone as a surprise.

The Runaway Mummy: A Petrifying Parody and Goodnight Goon: A Petrifying Parody by Michael Rex

"Once there was a little mummy who wanted to run away. 'If you run away,' said Mother Mummy, 'I will get you! For you are my rotten little mummy!'" If you are a child who read *The Runaway Bunny* (Brown 1942) recently, or a parent who has the words to the classic imprinted on your brain forever, you're already cracking up. Watching the little mummy change into different horrid creatures is pretty funny, as is the scariest creature he can think of . . . And there's also *Goodnight Goon*: "Goodnight skull/And goodnight shoe/Goodnight creature/Goodnight goo/And goodnight to the old werewolf hollering 'Boo.'" That's a perfect Halloween good-night story for any little monster, especially if you read it right after the original Margaret Wise Brown books. Or if you have kids prone to nightmares, you might want to read the parody first and then the classics, to have a sweet bunny as the lasting image that they carry with them to bed. That's what we do.

The 13 Days of Halloween by Carol Greene, illustrated by Tim Raglin

This book can be sung, to the tune of "The Twelve Days of Christmas." It's patterned on the traditional carol, but instead of "my true love," it is "my good friend" (a dashing ghoul) who gives his ghostly heartthrob a slew of hysterical—and pretty ghastly—gifts, like cooked worms, fat toads, and a vulture in a dead tree. On the 13th day, readers are invited to guess what she gives to her good friend when she invites him to tea. Although the story is silly fun, it is the illustrations that make this book such a hit with children. The drawings are intricate and detailed with tons of funny twists. The characters change costumes and turn up in new situations as the book progresses. For example, the six screeching owls might be balancing on the ghoul's arms on one page spread, yet you'll find them sipping through straws as they perch on the lip of a bubbling cauldron on another page.

Easter

Easter is a holiday much like Christmas in our house—not being religious people, we don't exactly celebrate the holiday as its origins might dictate. It's more of a "spring Halloween" at our house, where instead of orange and black, everything is pastel, and instead of trick-or-treating, the Easter Bunny just brings you a basket. To be perfectly honest, the whole fluffy bunnies and chicks thing kind of grates on my nerves. But since I'm also not a fan of a holiday that is purely about sugar and gifts and doesn't have room for books, we needed to find a way to make sure books were a big part of Easter. Without religious books or the baby animal books, how to do that? What we've decided to do is center the Easter basket on a book for each kid.

Having twins means that we're constantly asking them to share but also trying to encourage their own preferences and favorites and ownership. It also means we have to pay for everything in one fell swoop. (Time for big-kid beds? Need two of them. Ready for preschool? Two tuitions each month. Art class? Times two. New car seats . . . You get the picture.) So we try to balance out sharing and having their own with not going broke—which means we try to save in some little ways while making sure they carve out their own identities. When it comes to Christmas stockings, of course everyone gets their own. But Easter baskets a few months later? We share. One big basket is left on the table, and it's filled with replenishings of art supplies and one book gift for each kid. But since there is only one for each kid, and they're in the same basket, we have to be careful that the books aren't something they'll fight over. That eliminates things like a different Elephant and Piggie or Captain Underpants for each—I can guarantee that one of the books would be preferred and fought over. So we came up with a tradition where we think of a theme and give each kid a book that plays to his or her preferences within that theme.

The first year we did this, I wasn't particularly creative. We did the old Easter standby of bunnies and chicks—but I searched high and low for non-cutesy versions. In my head I called them badass bunny books, to make myself feel cooler. We got *Tough Chicks* by Cece Meng (2009) for Molly. Mom (Ruth) found this book for us, and it's wonderful. Penny, Polly, and Molly aren't your average chicks. They like mud and mess and figuring out how things work. They are some tough chicks, and Mama Hen is pretty darn proud of them. We got *Big Rabbit's Bad Mood* by Ramona Badescu (2009) for Jacob. We all continue to enjoy having a book to read when we're in a bad mood—especially since Big Mommy can always make it better.

The following year we did books based on favorite colors, since we knew they wouldn't fight over those. Molly has loved green and Jacob red since before they could even say the words.

Finally, for the most recent Easter, the kids were five and had just started taking lessons earlier in the year. We let them each pick one thing to take lessons in; Molly picked ballet, and Jacob picked golf. They adore those activities, and they especially love being the expert in the family on something. So there was no fighting at all when the Easter Bunny brought them activity-themed books.

Why This Matters

Marking the cycles of festivals and holidays is a thoughtful and meaningful way for children and families to appreciate the rhythms of the year.

The smell of holiday baking is different across the seasons. The rich feelings of warmth in front of the fire or in the glow of candlelight during winter holidays is markedly different from the spring celebration that honors new life outdoors with egg hunts. Children appreciate the safety of returning year after year to whatever traditions tie them to their family celebrations and their larger culture.

Building rituals into family holiday celebrations provides another way for children to connect to the cycles of the seasons and their place in the natural world. Educator Barbara Patterson (2000) writes movingly about the crucial roles of parents in helping make those connections for their families to rely on, focusing on the natural rhythms of the seasons. She argues that holiday celebrations have the power to reconnect to nature in a way that was more common when people depended upon the natural world for their daily existence: "When more people depended directly upon nature for their living, their lives were, of necessity, more rhythmic. They recognized that the rhythms of their days, their weeks, and even the seasons of the year supported them by yielding to them what they needed to live" (p. 53).

Like other traditions, holiday celebrations are the perfect vehicle to strengthen family identity, unity, and a feeling of security. The ceremonial nature—and special-occasion status—of these observances can add a special aura and excitement. Often, the extended family can take part, and special-occasion books

Photo 11-2: Grandpa reads to a group of cousins.

can play a wonderful role in bringing together families across generations. Books that are revisited yearly and read by different family members lend a new voice to traditional celebrations. Sharing new books as conversation starters can also be a kind of icebreaker for family members to reintroduce themselves when they haven't seen each other for a while. (See Photo 11-2.)

We think of the power of traditions and celebration as perfect vehicles to heighten *routines, relationships, and rhythms* in family environments. We hope the reading and celebration suggestions we've shared get you even more excited about weaving books into all your family rituals. We can't imagine our family traditions without books at the heart of them.

And the Beat Goes On

We chose the title of this book because in our minds, *home is where the heart is*, and for us that is inseparable from *books*. Stories woven into our special homey spaces; favorite characters informing our celebrations and everyday activities; letters, books, words, and symbols revealing their magic and power on a daily basis. From the time we first heard the tiny heartbeats of the littlest members of our family, we knew we wanted to create a home environment that reflected the rhythms of literacy. These six years have been exhilarating as we have learned from each other and most of all from the children in our lives—Molly and Jacob, of course, but as they grow older, from their friends and friends' families, and the larger community as well, as the twins become more a part of the world around them.

As the kids get older, the questions keep coming. Their world is changing in ways we can't even imagine or wrap our heads around. What new books, genres, and formats lie ahead as we get to grow as readers alongside Molly and Jacob? As we relive our second childhood through the books to come, we look forward to the journey.

You know what your family loves and needs. You know the rhythms of your life. We are comforted by the literate spaces we've carved into our home, energized by the world of choices in the books we read, and are looking forward to continued forays into the latest fascinating research in child development that informs us about why this matters. Our hope is that you'll find the stories and suggestions in this book a useful starting place that will take your literacy adventures in the directions they need to go. Be open to the new worlds that are ahead. And trust yourselves. Happy reading!

References

Burns, M. Susan, Peg Griffin, and Catherine Snow. 1999. *Starting Out Right: A Guide to Promoting Children's Reading Success*. Washington, DC: National Academies Press.

Bus, Adriana, Marion van Ijzendoorn, and Anthony Pellegrini. 1995. "Joint Book Reading Makes for Success in Learning to Read: A Meta-Analysis of Intergenerational Transmission of Literacy." *Review of Educational Research* 65 (1): 1–21.

Christian, Katherine, Frances Morrison, and Florence Bryant. 1998. "Predicting Kindergarten Academic Skills: Interactions Among Child Care, Maternal Education, and Family Literacy Environments." *Early Childhood Research Quarterly* 13 (3): 501–521.

Colker, Laura. 2009. "Literacy Development Begins at Home, with a Literate Home Environment." *The Children's Book Review*, September 8.

Dewar, Gwen. 2009. "The Effects of Television on Children Learning to Talk: Does TV Really Cause a Learning Lag in Babies?" *Parenting Science*. www.parentingscience.com/effects-of-television-on-children-learning-speech.html.

Dorsey, John. 2011. "When Do Babies See Color for the First Time?" *Babies Today*. www.babiestoday/expertqa/everyday-issues/when-do-babies-start-to-see-color-for-the-first-time-147/.

Ehri, Linnea C. 1994. "Development of the Ability to Read Words: Update." In *Theoretical Models and Processes of Reading*, 4th ed., ed. R. Ruddell and H. Singer. Newark, DE: International Reading Association.

Epstein, Ann. 2012. "Social-Emotional Development." In *Children of 2020: Creating a Better Tomorrow*, ed. V. Washington and J. D. Andrews. Washington, DC: National Association for the Education of Young Children.

Fiese, Barbara. 2006. *Family Routines and Rituals*. New Haven, CT: Yale University Press.

———. 2002. "A Review of 50 Years of Research on Naturally Occurring Family Routines and Rituals: Cause for Celebration?" *Journal of Family Psychology* 16 (4): 381–390.

Gillespie, Linda, and Sandra Peterson. 2012. "Rituals and Routines." *Young Children* 67 (4): 76–77.

Goleman, Daniel. 1992. "Study Finds Babies at Five Months Grasp Simple Mathematics." *New York Times*. August 27, www.nytimes.com/1992/08/27/us/study-finds-babies-at-5-months-grasp-simple-mathematics.html?src=pm.

Guernsey, Lisa. 2007. *Into the Minds of Babes: How Screen Time Affects Young Children from Birth to Age Five*. New York: Basic Books.

Jacobsen, Mary. 1982. "Looking for Literary Space: The Willing Suspension of Disbelief Revisited." *Research in the Teaching of English* 16 (1): 21–28.

Keene, Ellin, and Susan Zimmerman. 2007. *Mosaic of Thought*. Portsmouth, NH: Heinemann.

Patterson, Barbara. 2000. *Beyond the Rainbow Bridge: Nurturing Our Children from Birth to Seven*. Amesbury, MA: Michaelmas.

Pearson, P. David, Laura Roehler, Janice Doyle, and Gerry Duffy. 1992. "Developing Expertise in Reading Comprehension." In *What Research Has to Say About Reading Instruction*, ed. J. Samuels and A. Farstrup. Newark, DE: International Reading Association.

Rasinski, Timothy, and Anthony Fredericks. 1991. "The Second Best Advice for Parents." *The Reading Teacher* 44 (6): 438–439.

Reading Is Fundamental. "Creating a Reading Environment at Home." www.rif.org/us/literacy-resources/articles/literacy-development-begins-at-home.htm.

Rideout, Victoria, Elizabeth Vandewater, and Ellen Wartella. 2003. *Zero to Six: Electronic Media in the Lives of Infants, Toddlers, and Pre-schoolers*. A report prepared by the Henry J. Kaiser Family Foundation and the Children's Digital Media Centers. www.kff.org/entmedia/3378.cfm.

Roberts, Michelle. 2005. "Babies Have Favorite Colours." BBC News. Last updated May 8, 2005. http://news.bbc.co.uk/2/hi/health/4474725.stm.

Slomski, Anita. 2008. "Mirror, Mirror." *Proto: Dispatches from the Frontiers of Medicine.* http://protomag.com/assets/mirror-mirror?page=1.

Sophian, Charles. 2004. "Mathematics for the Future." *Early Childhood Research Quarterly* 19:59–81.

Stamm, Jill. 2008. *Bright from the Start.* New York: Gotham Books.

Talbot, Margaret. 2006. "The Baby Lab: How Elizabeth Spelke Peers into the Infant Mind." *The New Yorker.* www.newamerica.net/publications/articles/2006/the_baby_lab.

Tallal, Paula. 2004. "Improving Language and Literacy Is a Matter of Time." *Nature Reviews: Neuroscience* 5 (9): 721–728.

Wagner, Richard, and Joseph Torgensen. 1987. "The Nature of Phonological Processing and Its Causal Role in the Acquisition of Reading Skills." *Psychological Bulletin* 101 (2): 192–212.

Well, Gordon. 1985. *Language Development in the Pre-School Years.* Cambridge, England: Cambridge University Press.

Winerip, Michael. 2010. "A Father-Daughter Bond, Page by Page." *The New York Times* March 18. http://www.nytimes.com/2010/03/21/fashion/21GenB.html?pagewanted=all&_r=0

Children's Books

Alcott, Louisa May. (1868) 2012. *Little Women*. Los Angeles: Simon and Brown.
Andersen, Hans Christian, and Virginia Lee Burton. 2004. *The Emperor's New Clothes*. Torrance, CA: Sandpiper.
Angelou, Maya. (1969) 2009. *I Know Why the Caged Bird Sings*. New York: Ballantine Books.
Anonymous. (1971) 2005. *Go Ask Alice*. New York: Simon Pulse.
Atwater, Richard, and Florence Atwater. 1992. *Mr. Popper's Penguins*. New York: Little Brown.
Awdrey, Rev. W. 2010. *Thomas' ABC Book*. New York: Perfection Learning.
Azarian, Mary. (1981) 2012. *A Farmer's Alphabet*. Boston: Godine.
Badescu, Ramona. 2009. *Big Rabbit's Bad Mood*. San Francisco: Chronicle Books.
Baltazar, Franco, and Art Baltazar. 2009. *Tiny Titans: Welcome to the Treehouse*. New York: DC Comics.
Barton, Byron. 1991. *The Three Bears*. New York: HarperFestival.
Bee, William. 2009. *Beware of the Frog*. London: Walker Children's Paperbacks.
———. 2007. *And the Train Goes . . .* Somerville, MA: Candlewick.
———. 2005. *Whatever*. London: Walker Children's Paperbacks.
Berg, Brook. 2006. *When Marion Copied*. Madison, WI: Upstart Books.
———. 2005. *What Marion Taught Willis*. Madison, WI: Upstart Books.
———. 2003. *What Happened to Marion's Book?* Madison, WI: Upstart Books.

Blume, Judy. (1975) 2007. *Forever*. New York: Simon Pulse.
Bokova, Tatiana. 2007. *Azbooka—Russian ABC's— in Russian Language*. St. Paris, OH: Prof-Press.
Bray, Libba. 2005. *A Great and Terrible Beauty*. New York: Ember.
Brett, Jan. 2009. *The Mitten*. New York: Putnam Juvenile.
———. 2003a. *On Noah's Ark*. New York: Putnam.
———. 2003b. *Town Mouse, Country Mouse*. New York: Puffin.
———. 1995. *Armadillo Rodeo*. New York: Putnam.
Brown, Lisa. 2005. *Baby, Mix Me a Drink*. San Francisco: McSweeney's.
Brown, Margaret Wise. (1947) 2005. *Goodnight Moon*. New York: HarperCollins.
———. (1942) 2005. *The Runaway Bunny*. New York: HarperCollins.
Carpenter, Steve. 1998. *Dreidel, Dreidel, Dreidel Board Book*. New York: HarperFestival.
Carroll, Lewis. (1865) 1993. *Alice's Adventures in Wonderland*. Mineola, NY: Dover.
Cave, Kathryn. 2003. *One Child, One Seed: A South African Counting Book*. New York: Henry Holt.
Chbosky, Stephen. 2012. *The Perks of Being a Wallflower*. New York: MTV Books.
Cheng, Andrea. 2003. *Grandfather Counts*. New York: Lee & Low Books.
Child, Lauren. 2006a. *But Excuse Me That Is My Book*. Dial.
———. 2006b. *The Princess and the Pea*. New York: Hyperion.
———. 2003. *I Will Never Not Ever Eat a Tomato: Charlie and Lola*. Somerset, MA: Candlewick.
Cleary, Brian. 2006. *Peanut Butter and Jellyfishes: A Very Silly Alphabet Book*. Brookfield, CT: Millbrook.
Climo, Shirley. 2001. *The Persian Cinderella*. New York: HarperCollins.
Coburn, Jewell Reinhart. 1996. *Jouanah: A Hmong Cinderella*. Alhambra, CA: Shens Books and Supplies.
Cole, Babbette. 1997. *Prince Cinders*. New York: Puffin.
Coleman, Penny. 2008. *Thanksgiving: The True Story*. New York: Henry Holt.
Cooper, Helen. 2009. *Pumpkin Soup*. New York: MacMillan Young Readers.
Cormier, Robert. 2004. *The Chocolate War*. New York: Ember.
Coyle, Carmela LaVigna. 2003. *Do Princesses Wear Hiking Boots?* New York: Cooper Square.
Crowther, Robert. 2009. *Cars*. Somerset, MA: Candlewick.
Cuyler, Margery. 2005. *Skeleton Hiccups*. New York: Margaret K. Elderberry.

D'Agnese, Joseph. 2012. *Blockhead: The Life of Fibonacci.* New York: Henry Holt.
de Costa, Deborah. 2007. *Hannukah Moon.* Minneapolis, MN: Kar-Ben.
de Haan, Linda, and Stern Nijland. 2003. *King and King.* New York: Tricycle.
Demarest, Chris. 2003. *Firefighters A to Z.* New York: Margaret K. McElderry Books.
Dillon, Leo, and Dianne Dillon. 2007. *Jazz on a Saturday Night.* New York: Blue Sky.
Dodds, Dayle Ann. 2007. *Minnie's Diner: A Multiplying Menu.* Somerville, MA: Candlewick.
Dooley, Norah. 2004. *Everybody Serves Soup.* Minneapolis, MN: Carolrhoda Books.
———. 1995. *Everybody Bakes Bread.* Minneapolis, MN: Carolrhoda Books.
———. 1992. *Everybody Cooks Rice.* Minneapolis, MN: Carolrhoda Books.
Dr. Seuss. 2011. *The Bippolo Seed and Other Lost Stories.* New York: Random House Books for Young Readers.
——— 1996. *My Many Colored Days.* New York: Knopf Books for Young Readers.
——— (1957) 2007. *How the Grinch Stole Christmas!* New York: Random House Books for Young Readers.
Duncan, Lois. 2011. *Killing Mr. Griffen.* New York: Perfection Learning.
Eager, Edgar. 1999. *Knight's Castle.* Torrance, CA: Sandpiper.
Edwards, Michelle. 1992. *Alef-Bet: A Hebrew Alphabet Book.* New York: Lothrop, Lee and Shepard.
Elting, Mary, and Michael Folsom. 2005. *Q Is for Duck: An Alphabet Guessing Game.* San Anselmo, CA: Sandpiper Press.
Emberley, Rebecca. 2010. *The Red Hen.* New York: Roaring Brook.
Enzenberger, Hans Magnus. 2000. *The Number Devil: A Mathematical Adventure.* New York: Holt.
Ernst, Lisa Campbell. 2004. *The Turn-Around, Upside-Down Alphabet Book.* New York: Simon and Schuster.
Evans, Cambria. 2008. *Bone Soup.* Boston: Houghton Mifflin Books for Children.
Falconer, Ian. 2000. *Olivia.* New York: Atheneum Books for Young Readers.
Feffer, Kate. 2013. *Double Pink.* New York: Simon and Schuster.
Fosberry, Jennifer. 2010. *My Name Is Not Isabella.* Chicago: Sourcebooks Jabberwocky.

Fromental, Jean-Luc. 2006. 365 *Penguins*. New York: Abrams Books for Young Readers.
Funke, Cornelia. 2007. *Princess Pigsty*. Somerset, England: The Chicken House.
———. 2006. *Pirate Girl*. Somerset, England: The Chicken House.
Galdone, Paul. 2011. *The Three Bears* (Folk Tale Classics) Boston: Houghton Mifflin Harcourt Books.
Garcia, Emma. 2008. *Toot Toot Beep Beep*. New York: Boxer Books.
———. 2007. *Tip Tip Dig Dig*. New York: Boxer Books.
Gerstein, Mordecai. 2009. *A Book*. New York: Roaring Brook.
Gibbons, Gail. 2003. *Cowboys and Cowgirls: Yippee-Yay!* New York: Little, Brown Books for Young Readers.
Giganti, Paul. 1999. *Each Orange Had 8 Slices*. New York: Greenwillow Books.
Glasser, Linda. 1997. *The Borrowed Hanukkah Latkes*. Park Ridge, IL: Albert Whitman.
Gleeson, Brian. 1988. *Pecos Bill*. Read by Robin Williams. Westport, CT: Picture Book Studio Audio. Audiobook.
Golio, Gary. 2011. *When Bob Met Woody: The Story of the Young Bob Dylan*. New York: Little, Brown Books for Young Readers.
Gorbachev, Valeri. 2010. *What's the Big Idea, Molly?* New York: Philomel.
———. 2009. *Molly Who Flew Away*. New York: Philomel.
Grace, Catherine O'Neill. 2004. *1621: A New Look at Thanksgiving*. Des Moines, IA: National Geographic Children's Books.
Graham, Bob. 2006. *Max*. Frederick, MD: Walker Children's Paperbacks.
Greene, Carol. 2009. *The 13 Days of Halloween*. Naperville, IL: Sourcebooks Jabberwocky.
Hall, Donald. 1999. *String Too Short to Be Saved*. Boston: David R. Godine.
———. 1998. *The Man Who Lived Alone*. Boston: David R. Godine.
———. 1983. *Ox-Cart Man*. New York: Puffin USA.
Hamilton, Kersten. 2008. *Red Truck*. New York: Viking Juvenile.
Harris, Peter. 2007. *Night Pirates*. New York: Egmont Books.
Harris, Robie. 2009. *It's Perfectly Normal*. Somerville, MA: Candlewick.
Hartman, Deborah. 2004. *Jacob and the Magic Feather*. Charleston, SC: BookSurge.
Hawkes, Kevin. 2011. *The Wicked Big Toddlah Goes to New York*. New York: Knopf Books for Young Readers.
———. 2010. *The Wicked Big Toddlah*. New York: Dragonfly Books.
Heap, Sue. 2012. *Cowboy Baby*. Winter Park, FL: Walker.
Henkes, Kevin. 1996. *Lilly's Purple Plastic Purse*. New York: Greenwillow.

Hobbie, Nathaniel. 2008. *Priscilla and the Pink Planet*. New York: Little, Brown Books for Young Readers.
Hong, Lily Toy. 2007. *Two of Everything: A Chinese Folktale*. Newton, KS: Paw Prints.
Horowitz, Dave. 2011a. *Humpty Dumpty Climbs Again*. New York: Puffin.
———. 2011b. *Twenty-Six Princesses*. New York: Puffin.
———. 2009. *Duck Duck Moose*. New York: Putnam Juvenile.
———. 2007. *Five Little Gefiltes*. New York: Putnam Juvenile.
———. 2004. *A Monkey Among Us*. New York: Harper Festival.
Hughes, Langston. 1997. *The Sweet and Sour Animal Book*. New York: Oxford University Press, USA.
Isadora, Rachel. 2009a. *The Ugly Duckling*. New York: Putnam Juvenile.
———. 2009b. *Hansel and Gretel*. New York: Putnam Juvenile.
———. 2008. *Rapunzel*. New York: Putnam Juvenile.
———. 2007. *The Princess and the Pea*. New York: Putnam Juvenile.
Jackson, Ellen. 1998. *Cinder Edna*. New York: HarperCollins.
Jay, Alison. 2003. *ABC: A Child's First Alphabet Book*. New York: Dutton Juvenile Books.
Johnson, Stephen T. 2003. *City by Numbers*. London: Puffin.
Juma, Siddiqa. 2000. *My First Arabic Alphabet Book*. New York: Tahrike Tarsile Quran.
Kann, Elizabeth, and Victoria Kann. 2006. *Pinkalicious*. New York: HarperCollins.
Kahora, Kazuno. 2010. *Ghosts in the House!* New York: Square Fish.
———. 2009. *Here Comes Jack Frost*. New York: Roaring Brook.
Kaplan, Bruce Eric. 2010. *Monsters Eat Whiny Children*. New York: Simon and Schuster.
Keller, Holly. 1999. *Jacob's Tree*. New York: Greenwillow Books.
Ketteman, Helen. 1997. *Bubba, the Cowboy Prince*. New York: Scholastic.
Kimmel, Eric A. 2008. *Little Britches and the Rattlers*. Charlotte, NC: Amazon Children's Publishing.
Kimmelman, Leslie. 2010. *The Little Red Hen and the Passover Matzah*. New York: Holiday House.
Kirk, Daniel. 2009. *Library Mouse: A Friend's Tale*. New York: Harry N. Abrams.
———. 2007. *Library Mouse*. New York: Harry N. Abrams.
Kochalka, James. 2008. *Johnny Boo: The Best Little Ghost in the World*. Marietta, GA: Top Shelf Productions.
Krakauer, Jon. 2011. *Three Cups of Deceit*. Harpswell, ME: Anchor.
Krauss, Ruth. 1960. *The Carrot Seed*. New York: Scholastic Books.

Krosoczka, Jarrett J. 2010. *Punk Farm*. New York: Dragonfly Books.
———. 2006. *Giddy Up, Cowgirl*. New York: Viking Juvenile.
———. 2003. *Bubble Bath Pirates*. New York: Viking Juvenile.
Krull, Kathleen, and Paul Brewer. 2008. *Fartiste*. New York: Simon and Schuster.
Kunhardt, Dorothy. (1940) 2001. *Pat the Bunny*. New York: Golden Books.
Lee, Harper. (1950) 2010. *To Kill a Mockingbird*. New York: Harper.
Lee, Huy Van. 2000. *In the Snow*. New York: Henry Holt.
———. 1998a. *At the Beach*. New York: Square Fish.
———. 1998b. *In the Park*. New York: Henry Holt.
Lee, Suzy. 2008. *Wave*. San Francisco: Chronicle Books.
Lee, Tae-Joon. 2007. *Waiting for Mama*. New York: NorthSouth Books.
L'Engle, Madeleine. 2010. *The Twenty-Four Days Before Christmas*. New York: Farrar, Strauss and Giroux.
———. (1962) 2012. *A Wrinkle in Time*. New York: Farrar, Strauss, and Giroux.
Lenski, Lois. (1945) 2005. *Strawberry Girl*. New York: HarperCollins.
———. 2000a. *The Little Fire Engine*. New York: Random House Books for Young Readers.
———. 2000b. *The Little Train*. New York: Random House Books for Young Readers.
Lester, Helen. 2005. *Tacky in Trouble*. Torrance, CA: Sandpiper.
———. 1990. *Tacky the Penguin*. Torrance, CA: Sandpiper.
Lies, Brian. 2008. *Bats at the Library*. Boston: Houghton Mifflin Books for Children.
———. 2006. *Bats at the Beach*. Boston: Houghton Mifflin Books for Children.
Lindgren, Astrid. (1945) 2005. *Pippi Longstocking*. New York: Puffin.
Litwin, Eric. 2011. *Pete the Cat: Rocking in My School Shoes*. New York: HarperCollins.
———. 2010. *Pete the Cat: I Love My White Shoes*. New York: HarperCollins.
Lewis, C. S. (1950) 2009. *The Lion, the Witch, and the Wardrobe*. New York: HarperCollins.
Lionni, Leo. 1968. *The Alphabet Tree*. New York: Knopf Books for Young Readers.
Lobel, Arnold. 1984. *Days with Frog and Toad*. Des Moines, IA: Perfection Learning.
Long, Melinda. 2007. *Pirates Don't Change Diapers*. New York: Harcourt Children's Books.
———. 2003. *How I Became a Pirate*. New York: Harcourt.

Lopresti, Angeline Sparagna, and Phyllis Hornung. 2003. *A Place for Zero: A Math Adventure.* Watertown, MA: Charlesbridge.
Louie, Al-Ling. 1996. *Yeh-Shen: A Cinderella Story from China.* New York: Puffin.
Lowell, Susan. 2001. *Cindy Ellen: A Wild Western Cinderella.* New York: HarperCollins.
Lowry, Lois. 1993. *The Giver.* Boston: Houghton Mifflin.
Mado, Michio. 1998. *The Magic Pocket.* New York: Margaret K. McElderry.
Manitonquat. 1994. *The Children of the Morning Light: Wampanoag Tales as Told by Manitonquat.* New York: Simon and Schuster.
Mansbach, Adam. 2011. *Go the F**k to Sleep.* New York: Akashic Books.
Mayer, Marianna. 1994. *Baba Yaga and Vasilisa the Brave.* New York: HarperCollins.
McBratney, Sam. (1994) 2008. *Guess How Much I Love You.* Somerville, MA: Candlewick.
McCloskey, Robert. (1948) 2010. *Blueberries for Sal.* New York: Puffin Books USA.
———. (1941) 1999. *Make Way for Ducklings.* New York: Puffin Books USA.
McConnell, Sarah. 2006. *Don't Mention Pirates.* Hauppauge, NY: Barron's Educational Series.
McLeod, Bob. 2008. *Superhero ABC.* New York: HarperCollins.
McPhail, David. 1997. *Edward and the Pirates.* New York: Little, Brown Books for Young Readers.
Meng, Cece. 2009. *Tough Chicks.* New York: Clarion Books.
Meyer, Stephanie. 2008. *Twilight.* New York: Little, Brown Books for Young Readers.
Micklethwait, Lucy. 1998. *I Spy Two Eyes: Numbers in Art.* New York: Greenwillow Books.
Moore, Clement. (1837) 2002. *'Twas the Night Before Christmas.* Somerville, MA: Candlewick.
Mora, Pat. 2000. *Tomas and the Library Lady.* New York: Dragonfly Books.
———. 1997. *Tomas y la Senora de la Biblioteca.* New York: Dragonfly Books.
Morales, Yuyi. 2008. *Just in Case: A Trickster Tale and Spanish Alphabet Book.* New York: Roaring Brook.
Morrison, Toni. 1994. *The Bluest Eye.* New York: Plume/Penguin.
Mortensen, Greg. 2009. *Listen to the Wind.* New York: Dial.
———. 2007. *Three Cups of Tea.* Des Moines, IA: Perfection Learning.
Munsch, Robert N. 1992. *The Paperbag Princess.* Toronto, ON: Annick.

Muth, Jon. 2010. *Zen Ghosts*. New York: Scholastic.
———. 2008. *Zen Ties*. New York: Scholastic.
———. 2005. *Zen Shorts*. New York: Scholastic.
Myers, Walter Dean. 2008. *Fallen Angels*. New York: Scholastic.
Myracle, Lauren. 2005. *ttyl* (series). New York: Amulet Books.
Naylor, Phyllis Reynolds. 2003. *Simply Alice* (Alice Books). New York: Simon Pulse Books.
Nelson, James L. 2004. *The Only Life That Mattered: The Short and Merry Lives of Ann Bonny, Mary Read, and Calico Jack Rackam*. Ithaca, NY: McBooks.
Nesbitt, Edith. (1906) 2012. *The Railway Children*. New York: Oxford University Press, USA.
Neuschwander, Cindy. 2009. *Mummy Math: An Adventure in Geometry*. New York: Square Fish.
Nicoll, Holly. 2012. *Meg and Mog*. London: Puffin.
Niffenegger, Audrey. 2010. *Her Fearful Symmetry*. New York: Scribner.
Norton, Mary. (1952) 2003. *The Borrowers*. Torrance, CA: Sandpiper.
O'Connor, Jane. 2005. *Fancy Nancy*. New York: HarperCollins.
O'Neill, Mary. 1990. *Hailstones and Halibut Bones*. New York: Doubleday Books for Young Readers.
Otoshi, Kathryn. 2010. *Zero*. Berkeley, CA: KO Kids Books.
———. 2008. *One*. Berkeley, CA: KO Kids Books.
Pearson, Deborah. 2003. *Alphabeep! A Zipping Zooming ABC*. New York: Holiday House.
Pfister, Marcus. 1994. *Penguin Pete*. New York: North-South Books.
———. 1992. *The Rainbow Fish*. New York: North-South Books.
Pilkey, Dav. 2002. *Captain Underpants*. New York: Blue Sky.
Pinczes, Elinor J. 2002. *A Remainder of One*. Torrance, CA: Sandpiper Books.
Pinto, Sarah. 2003. *The Alphabet Room*. New York: Bloomsbury USA Children's Books.
Piper, Watty. (1930) 1976. *The Little Engine That Could*. New York: Platt & Munk.
Potter, Beatrix. (1904) 2002. *The Tale of Two Bad Mice*. New York: Warne.
———. (1902) 2002. *The Tale of Peter Rabbit*. New York: Warne.
Primavera, Elise. 1999. *Auntie Claus*. New York: Silver Whistle.
Pullman, Phillip. 2011. His Dark Materials. (series) New York: Everyman's Library.
Raschka, Chris. 2003. *Mysterious Thelonious*. Palo Alto, CA: Live Oak.
Recorvits, Helen. 2003. *My Name Is Yoon*. New York: Farrar, Straus and Giroux.

Rex, Michael. 2009. *The Runaway Mummy: A Petrifying Parody*. New York: Putnam Juvenile.

———. 2008. *Goodnight Goon: A Petrifying Parody*. New York: Putnam Juvenile.

Richardson, Justin, and Peter Parnell. 2005. *And Tango Makes Three*. New York: Simon and Schuster.

Rickards, Lynn. 2010. *Jacob O'Reilly Wants a Pet*. Hauppauge, NY: Barron's Educational Series.

Rosenthal, Amy Krouse. 2009. *Yes Day*. New York: HarperCollins.

Rouss, Silvia. 1993. *Sammy Spider's First Hanukkah*. Minneapolis, MN: Kar-Ben.

Rowling, J. K. 1999. *Harry Potter and the Sorcerer's Stone, Book 1*. New York: Scholastic Paperbacks.

Runton, Andy. 2011. *Owly & Wormy: Friends All Aflutter*. New York: Atheneum Books for Young Readers.

———. 2004. *Owly*. Marietta, GA: Top Shelf Productions.

Rusch, Elizabeth. 2007. *A Day with No Crayons*. Flagstone, AZ: Rising Moon.

Salinger, J. D. (1951) 2001. *Catcher in the Rye*. New York: Back Bay Books.

San Souci, Robert D. 2002. *Cendrillon: A Caribbean Cinderella*. New York: Aladdin.

Schachner, Judy. 2010. *Skippyjon Jones*. Des Moines, IA: Perfection Learning.

Schroeder, Alan. 2000. *Smoky Mountain Rose: An Appalachian Cinderella*. New York: Puffin.

Schwartz, Alvin. 2010. *Scary Stories to Tell in the Dark*. New York: HarperCollins.

Schwartz, Richard Evan. 2010. *You Can Count on Monsters*. Natick, MA: AK Peters.

Schwarz, Viviane. 2010. *There Are No Cats in This Book*. Somerset, MA: Candlewick.

———. 2008a. *Timothy and the Strong Pajamas*. New York: Arthur A. Levine Books.

———. 2008b. *There Are Cats in This Book*. Somerset, MA: Candlewick.

Scieszka, Jon. 1995. *Math Curse*. New York: Viking Juvenile.

Scott, Walter. (1820) 2011. *Ivanhoe*. Frankfort, IL: Empire Books.

Seeger, Laura Vaccaro. 2007. *First the Egg*. New York: Roaring Brook.

Seeger, Pete. 2009. *Where Have All the Flowers Gone: A Singalong Memoir*. New York: W. W. Norton.

Segal, Eliezer. 1999. *Uncle Eli's Passover Haggadah*. San Francisco: No Starch.

Sendak, Maurice. 1991. *Alligators All Around: An Alphabet*. New York: HarperCollins.
———. 1991. *Pierre*. New York: HarperCollins.
———. 1986. *Maurice Sendak's Really Rosie Starring the Nutshell Kids*. New York: HarperCollins.
———. (1970) 1996. *In the Night Kitchen*. New York: HarperCollins.
———. (1963) 1988. *Where the Wild Things Are*. New York: HarperCollins.
Shahan, Sherry. 2007. *Spicy Hot Colors*. Atlanta: August House.
Shakespeare, William. (1623) 2004. *A Midsummer Night's Dream*. Washington, DC: Folger Shakespeare Library.
Shannon, David. 2004. *A Bad Case of Stripes*. New York: Scholastic.
———. 1998. *No, David!* New York: Blue Sky.
Sis, Peter. 2000. *Trucks, Trucks, Trucks*. New York: Scholastic Books.
Slade, Christian, and Ann Slade. 2007. *Korgi*. Marietta, GA: Top Shelf Productions.
Smith, Lane. 2011. *Grandpa Green*. New York: Roaring Brook.
Sobel, June. 2009. *Shiver Me Letters: A Pirate ABC*. Torrance, CA: Sandpiper.
———. 2006. *The Goodnight Train*. New York: Harcourt Brace.
Soman, David, and Jacky Davis. 2009. *Ladybug Girl and Bumblebee Boy*. New York: Dial Press.
———. 2008. *Ladybug Girl*. New York: Dial Press.
Squires, Janet. 2006. *Gingerbread Cowboy*. New York: HarperCollins.
Steinbeck, John. (1937) 1983. *Of Mice and Men*. New York: Bantam Books.
Stephens, Sarah. 2011. *Pooches of Power: DC Super-Pets!* Mankota, MN: Picture Window Books.
Steptoe, John. 2008. *Mufaro's Beautiful Daughters*. New York: Picture Puffin.
Stone, Jon. 2004. *The Monster at the End of the Book*. New York: Golden Books.
Swamp, Chief Jake. 1997. *Giving Thanks: A Native American Good Morning Message*. New York: Lee and Low Books.
Thayer, Jane. 2008. *The Blueberry Pie Elf*. Cynthiana, KY: Purple House Press.
Thomas, Dylan. (1950) 2003. *A Child's Christmas in Wales*. New York: New Directions.
Thompson, Kay. (1955) 1969. *Eloise*. New York: Simon and Schuster.
Travers, P. L. (1934) 2006. *Mary Poppins*. New York: Harcourt Children's Books.

Tucker, Kathy. 1997. *Do Pirates Take Baths?* Park Ridge, IL: Albert Whitman.
Twain, Mark. (1884) 1994. *The Adventures of Huckleberry Finn.* New York: Dover.
Van Allsburg, Chris. 2009. *The Polar Express.* Boston: Houghton Mifflin.
von Ziegesar, Cecily. 2002. Gossip Girl (series). Amherst, MA: Poppy.
Walker, Alice. (1982) 2003. *The Color Purple.* Boston: Mariner Books.
Walsh, Ellen Stoll. 1995. *Mouse Paint.* San Anselmo, CA: Sandpaper.
Walsh, Vivian. 1997. *Olive, the Other Reindeer.* San Francisco: Chronicle Books.
Waters, Kate. 2008. *Sarah Morton's Day: A Day in the Life of a Pilgrim Girl.* New York: Scholastic.
———. *Tapenum's Day: A Wampanoag Indian Boy in Pilgrim Times.* New York: Scholastic.
Weitzman, Jacqueline Preiss. 2001. *You Can't Take a Balloon into the Metropolitan Museum.* London: Puffin.
Wellington, Monica. 2006. *Mr. Cookie Baker.* New York: Dutton Juvenile.
Wells, Rosemary. 2000. *Max's Chocolate Chicken.* New York: Puffin USA.
Werner, Sharon, and Sarah Forss. 2009. *Alphabeasties: And Other Amazing Types.* Maplewood, NJ: Blue Apple Books.
Wilder, Laura Ingalls. (1932) 1981. *Little House in the Big Woods.* New York: HarperTrophy.
Willems, Mo. 2010. *We Are in a Book!* New York: Hyperion Books.
Williams, Jeffery. 2007. *Pirate Spirit: The Adventures of Anne Bonney.* Bloomington, IN: iUniverse.
Williams, Rozanne Lanczak. 2001. *The Coin Counting Book.* Watertown, MA: Charlesbridge.
Wise, William. 2004. *Ten Sly Piranhas.* London: Puffin.
Wisniewski, Dave. 1999. *Tough Cookie.* New York: HarperCollins.
Yarrow, Peter. 2009. *The Peter Yarrow Songbook: Let's Sing Together!* New York: Sterling.
Yolen, Jane. 1998. *The Ballad of the Pirate Queens.* New York: Voyager Books.
Zanes, Dan. 2004. *Hello Hello.* New York: Little, Brown Young Readers.
Ziefert, Harriet. 2010. *Passover: Celebrating Now, Remembering Then.* Maplewood, NJ: Blue Apple Books.
———. 2008a. *Hanukkah Haiku.* Maplewood, NJ: Blue Apple Books.
———. 2008b. *Mighty Max.* Maplewood, NJ: Blue Apple Books.
Zochert, Donald. 1977. *The Life of Laura Ingalls Wilder.* New York: Avon.

www.ingramcontent.com/pod-product-compliance
Lightning Source LLC
Chambersburg PA
CBHW071424160426
43195CB00013B/1805